Saving Your Financial Soul

A Modern Money Parable

Financial Soul Institute Publishing

Dedicated to my sister Maria
and my nephew Terrance
- *Brian Edward Ayers*

Dedicated to my mother Edith May Brooks
and my wife Michell
- *Alphonso Brooks*

Saving Your Financial Soul

A Modern Money Parable

Financial Soul Institute Publishing

Why I Wrote This Book

This book came about really because I had no choice. I needed to get out of my head the trap that I fell into years ago playing basketball that stayed with me well into my careers at AT&T, Department of Commerce, FEMA, NIH and running two businesses.

As a kid, I loved playing basketball and of course my biggest nemesis on the court was my big brother. I would get so caught up in being competitive and scoring that I would loose track of the score. So he kept the score.

After a while it started becoming obvious that he would add or subtract a basket when necessary for him to win. I don't blame him now because that's what big brothers do. But at the time it lead to some screaming matches and ugly two hour long games.

Needless to say I finally figured it out and I kept score too.

Unfortunately, I did not heed the lesson when I became an adult. Somehow I managed to have great paying jobs and even better businesses but still managed to stay broke.

How was this possible? I got the jobs as instructed and even rebelled to start my own dot com like any annually broke and fed up employee would. Still the money kept leaving.

Then I noticed that everyone I knew lived like this. I mean literally everyone! It was like we were all pre-programmed to never have enough and work for our entire lives for a fading hope of retiring.

Nobody was taught how to keep score.

So I did the research and realized that my financial soul was not operating in its own self interest. It had been hoodwinked, bamboozled and lead astray. This story shares a lot about what I have learned and it needed to be let out by any means necessary.

PS

My brother hasn't beaten me in a basketball game in a loooong time. (Yeah...I said it!)

Table of Contents

Your Financial Soul

Plato considered the soul to be the essence of a person that decides how we behave. While many people consider the soul in purely spiritual terms, in the physical world, finances dictate a great deal of how we behave. If you look around the room you are in right now, everything in it cost money except, of course, the people.

Money is an inescapable part of our lives. How we relate to it, think about it, spend it and work for it deserves study to the level of devotion. Although money is not worthy of praise, it is what drives millions of people worldwide to be away from their families the vast majority of their lives.

In truth, our financial soul is intertwined with our spiritual soul. It is even alluded to in the 10 Commandments. Stealing is very much an economic issue.

It is unwise to ignore this vital part of your earthly existence
for money is not the root of all evil…ignorance is.

Chapter 1

The Worker, the Builder & the Joker

The elevator came to a smooth stop with a distinctive ring on the 20th floor. Ed and Sasha took in the elaborate details on the elevator doors as they quietly slid open. The next thing they saw made no sense.

"Uh…are you sure they said the 20th floor", Ed asked as they stepped out looking to the left and right.

Sasha glanced up at the digital elevator sign flashing 20 as she followed Ed off. "That is what the office directory said downstairs and that is what is on our directions", she replied.

The 20th floor did not match the beautiful open architecture of the building or the ornate lobby. It was a huge open area with fluorescent light fixtures dangling from the ceiling and random piles of junk lightly coated in white dust all over the place. There was no carpet and they could hear the light crunch of dirt on the bare floor as they walked around.

"Maybe they moved offices", Sasha guessed.

Seemingly out of nowhere a booming voice came. "How are you folks doing?"

Ed's head snapped around as he said, "Woah…hey…didn't see you there."

A middle aged man with light sprinkles of grey in his hair was standing next to a janitors cart wearing a blue jump suit. His 5 foot 8 frame was filled out with the build of a man who worked out in between some good meals.

"I didn't mean to startle you" he said with a light chuckle. "Not too many people visit this floor anymore."

"We can tell" said Sasha. "We were looking for two gentlemen on this floor. Do you happen to know a Mr. Simmons or a Mr. Roberts?"

"I know both and I am one. I'm Simmons, Reverend Simmons that is" he answered.

"Wow, I mean…uh…Hi. I'm Ed Bagley and this is Sasha Brown. We are new to the Wealth Education Institute and we were sent here to meet our two mentors. But I am a little confused…

"No need to be confused son. You guys are at the right place at the right time as you always are. I am glad to meet both of you. Why don't we head down to my office?"

Rev. Simmons wheeled around and started walking down the remnants of a hallway. Ed and Sasha both got a sinking feeling. They were looking forward to talking with millionaire businessmen who would give them the secrets to making their millions. Now they were following a janitor down a bare hallway.

Toward the end of the hall, Rev. Simmons opened a non-descript door and slipped the janitors cart inside.

"No need to waste time. Why don't we head over to Mr. Roberts' office so we can all get a chance to know each other?" Once again, Sasha and Ed were off down the hall trying to keep up with Rev. Simmons' quick pace.

They stopped again in front of another non-descript door but this time it actually said Janitors Closet on the door. Rev. Simmons suddenly said, "Hold on a second" as he quickly pushed the door open, waited a second and then stepped in. "You gotta watch this guy", he whispered. "He is something of a practical joker."

Sasha and Ed followed him into a medium sized room that had janitors equipment laid out like it just came from the store. Untouched mops and brooms hung from racks on the wall. Empty yellow buckets were tucked into the corners. The room smelled surprisingly sterile with the lingering hint of cigar.

"This way", Rev. Simmons quietly urged as he headed to another door that looked like it headed to nowhere. Sasha and Ed just looked at each other as they crept along behind Rev. Simmons like they were breaking into the place.

Once again, he pushed open the door, waited a second and stepped in. As Sasha and Ed followed their mouths just opened in amazement. This room was absolutely gorgeous, large and had sweeping views of the surrounding office complex.

"Ok. Now I am completely confused" Ed stammered.

"Yeah and you look like it too" yelled a baritone voice almost directly into Ed's ear.

Ed jumped sideways bumping into the oversized leather sofa next to the door and almost fell on the floor.

Rev. Simmons and a huge bear of a man in the doorway started laughing like two third grade boys. Sasha stepped over to help Ed as he gathered himself.

"Oh that was a good one", Rev. Simmons managed in between laughs. "Please forgive us."

"Speak for yourself Rev. That was hysterical", laughed the white haired man. He had the build of a former NFL linebacker. His silk tie, expensive shirt and tailor made pants were accentuated by four huge diamond encrusted rings on his gigantic hands. It was not hard to tell who the millionaire in the room was.

"What is going on here?" asked Sasha with a bit of irritation in her voice.

"We have to have a little fun hazing our new students. I mean we only do this for fun", explained Rev. Simmons.

"Speak for yourself Rev. I'm in it for the tax breaks and some friendly victimization. I'm Mr. Roberts. You can call me Mr. Roberts. Why don't you guys have a seat?"

"Thanks", replied Ed as he continued looking around the room. As they made their way across the room they could feel the plush carpet underfoot. They sat down in comfortable seats around a well crafted low glass table. Every detail of the room screamed expensive. Mr. Roberts' desk sat in the corner facing the room with immaculate wood work and gold inlay on the sides. The floor to ceiling windows made the desk seem even larger and more surreal. In front of the desk was a large ornate R in white that stood out against the dark red carpeting.

"This is a wonderful office" said Sasha. I just don't understand why your office is hidden in the corner of an empty floor."

"Can't tell you that. I don't know if you guys are spies", replied Mr. Roberts.

"No spies here. We just want to live like this", murmured Ed.

"Careful what you ask for. Isn't that right Rev?" Mr. Roberts said with a wink. "Who wants something to drink?" he asked while moving to a well stocked mirrored bar in the back of the room with a flat TV behind it silently playing MSNBC.

"I would remind you that it is 11 o'clock in the morning but I know it is Happy Hour somewhere in your world", said the Reverend.

"You are right on both counts. So that means you guys can wait until later", he chuckled as he expertly made himself a martini.

"So let's get down to business", said Mr. Roberts as he carefully selected an olive. "Why are you here and what do you want?"

"Uh…we are here for the mentor program through The Wealth Education Institute", answered Ed. "They said you guys had a week long course on how to become millionaires."

"Ha! This ain't no millionaire course here son" said Mr. Roberts feigning a heavy southern drawl. "This here is money boot camp."

"What he meant to say is that these are not how to lessons but why lessons", answered Rev. Simmons.

"Yeah. Like why are you broke? Why is everyone you know broke? Why doesn't anyone know why they are broke? And why do I stay rich with half a college football scholarship education while my doctor works 10 hours a day and is $70,000 in debt", teased Mr. Roberts.

"That is because he needs that much time to figure out what is wrong with you and you keep trying to stiff him on the check", Rev. Simmons teased back. "What we will do over the next week is give you a crash course on what you should have learned every day of your life. Since you are here for help, I can guess that you guys are one of the broke folks Mr. Roberts spoke of."

"We are not broke" interrupted Ed. "We are just not wealthy."

"Can you guys be out of work for the next 3 months without being financially crippled?" snapped Mr. Roberts.

"Well..um", said Ed looking quizzically at Sasha who shrugged her shoulders.

"Broke", shouted both mentors together and started laughing.

"I'm sorry. We have made some assumptions about you guys without really getting to know you", said Rev. Simmons. "Why don't you guys formally introduce yourselves and tell us your story?"

"Sure", Sasha said brightly. "My name is Sasha Brown and this is my fiancé Ed Bagley. I am a contractor with the US government working in IT. I have read dozens of books on how to save money and make money but it just doesn't seem to be enough. I max my 401K, invest in stocks, save money, stay out of the stores and I have a condo in a run down part of town to keep cost low and be ready to sell when the area picks up on property value.

"But somehow it just doesn't seem like enough. I often wonder if I will ever become a millionaire. I see other people with nice cars and houses and I wonder if I will ever be like them. I know something must be missing…I just don't know what it is.

"It seems you are very close to what you want", replied Rev. Simmons. "If you went to a financial planner, they would tell you that you are exactly where you are supposed to be and to do more of the same."

"Then they would charge you to tell you how to gamble with it. I wish someone would pay me to make educated bets" added Mr. Roberts. "What about you son? What is your millionaire dream?"

"I have been working my internet business for the last 7 years. I have made hundreds of thousands of dollars but somehow the money seems to slip right through my fingers. I always wanted to have my own business but not so I can work even harder than I did for someone else for more stress and less pay."

"I have studied all aspects of business and have applied most of them but things aren't sticking. Before I start looking for more investors, I want to figure out where is the hole in my ship. I feel like I should have been successful a long time ago."

"Uh-oh partner", Rev Simmons said to Mr. Roberts. "This is going to be a tough one to crack right here."

"Maybe not. How quickly can you guys become idiots?" asked Mr. Roberts.

"What?" Sasha looked back and forth between the two older gentlemen.

"You guys are like a lot of people…sitting right on the bubble of wealth", explained Rev. Simmons. "All it takes are income sources and the right education to make a million dollars. The reason why you don't have it now is simply because you got the wrong financial education.

"Most people have been given the dependency education. You were told to get an education and get a job or in Ed's case to start your own business. Both fall way short of showing you the way to financial freedom. It is better for many companies if you are dependent on credit cards, loans and mortgages so you can continuously pay them for your existence. They have no reason to point out that there are ways to pay them hundreds of thousands of dollars less over your lifetime.

The Reverend sighed and continued. "The education system just simply moves slowly to adopt real financial education. It may be because the majority of people, including teachers, don't know what to teach because they are in the same trap."

"Don't forget it is easier for employers to keep the masses dumb so they keep coming back to work for a paycheck as long as they are needed", chuckled Mr. Roberts. "Ask me how I know."

"Even that causes problems for the companies but we are getting ahead of ourselves" said Rev. Simmons. "This is just the meet and greet session. The real work starts next week."

"Good. I am getting hungry, I have a trip to get moving on and I have to check on the cattle" said Mr. Roberts while finishing off his martini.

Rev. Simmons just looked at Mr. Roberts and sighed. "Do you guys have any questions?"

"Yes. What should we expect next week?" Sasha inquired.

"A whole world of hurt. I mean a complete money spanking the likes of which…" Mr. Roberts started.

"What he means", Rev Simmons interjected, "is there are going to be some things that will shake what you have always believed financially. You will need to keep an open mind and take notes.

"No, what I meant was a whole world of hurt with a money spanking", finished Mr. Roberts.

Rev. Simmons said, "Unfortunately, I will not be in on Monday so you will be at the mercy of Drill Sergeant Roberts here."

"Mercy? Ain't no mercy here", said Mr. Roberts as he kept his southern drawl going.

Chapter 2

The Industrial Age Paycheck

Monday morning at 9:55, Ed and Sasha stepped off the elevator on the 20th floor to see even more office junk scattered around the barren office landscape. With no one there to greet them, they headed over to Mr. Roberts' office.

They followed the same routine Rev. Simmons used. Ed pushed the first door open quickly and peeked in while Sasha made sure no one was behind them. With no practical jokes present they proceeded to knock on non-descript door number 2.

After knocking several times with no answer Ed opened the unlocked door and looked in only to see Mr. Roberts laying face down on the floor with an empty liquor bottle next to him. On seeing him on the floor Sasha dashed across the room and kneeled next to Mr. Roberts and began shaking his massive frame as much as she could.

"Oh my God. Mr. Roberts...are you OK? Ed come here and check to see if he is breathing", she exclaimed. "Do you think we should call someone?" She looked up at Ed and realized he had not moved from the door way and had a crooked grin on his face.

Suddenly Mr. Roberts yelled out loud and jumped up much faster than his size would suggest he could move. Sasha fell backwards on the plush carpet and screamed "Aaagh, I should have known it."

Mr. Robert's deep laugh filled the room while Ed walked over to help Sasha up. "I sort of saw that one coming," Sasha said. "A guy his size would have needed two bottles of liquor to knock him out."

"Oh man," Mr. Roberts said still laughing while holding his head. "I haven't played possum in years. That is the oldest trick in the book. I appreciate your concern. Now I just know not to have a heart attack around Ed. That actually hurt my head. It is still killing me from the weekend and the flight. You guys sit down. I gotta find some headache medicine."

"Serves you right," Sasha fired back.

"Don't be mad. I had to haze you too. Otherwise it would be sexist," replied Mr. Roberts.

Mr. Roberts sat down with Ed and Sasha. He popped two pills into his mouth and guzzled a full glass of water he grabbed from the bar.

"Here is a good thing to remember. Never gamble in Vegas and drink a shot every time you lose. I must have lost $5000 this weekend. Hanging with those high stakes sons of…"

Mr. Roberts shot a glance over at Sasha and then continued. "I mean high rolling gentlemen I call friends may not be good for your health but man is it fun."

"Wow! You are really living the life", replied Ed.

"There has to be some benefit to not being married and having no kids", Mr. Roberts said. "No offense little lady."

"None taken", Sasha replied. "So what are we in for today?"

"Today you get the grand tour of my empire. Or at least the part that is in this building. I want you guys to get an understanding of how I built my wealth. Then we can start picking it apart. Sound fair?"

Ed and Sasha nodded in agreement.

"I have several calls to get placed this morning so I am going to leave you with one of my floor managers to give you the grand tour. She can show you the cattle in their full glory", Mr. Roberts said. "This way kids".

Ed and Sasha followed Mr. Roberts out of a door next to the bar and found themselves in a staircase.

"This is how I get my exercise", exclaimed Mr. Roberts. "Only nine flights up. I hope you guys can keep up". Then he took off up the stairs.

Sasha looked at Ed who just rolled his eyes. "This is getting weirder all the time," Ed muttered under his breath as they chased Mr. Roberts up the steps.

At the 29th floor landing Mr. Roberts stopped and cracked the door open, peaked in and then walked through quickly with Ed and Sasha in tow. The 29th floor was as packed with cubicles and office furniture as the 20th floor was empty. There was a low level of office white noise as phones rang, conversations went on and printers and copiers churned away.

As they made their way through a labyrinth of hallways and cubicles, it was easy to see groups of people stop their conversations and scatter like high school kids who were up to something and Mr. Roberts was the principle.

Several people ducked or started walking the other way. One person just hung up the phone in mid sentence as Mr. Roberts walked past her cubicle. As they approached the manager's office, a thirty-ish looking woman with light blonde hair sitting in a cubicle offered a "Good morning Mr. Roberts."

With barely a glance, Mr. Roberts responded flatly, "Good morning Michelle. Glad you could make it in today. Tell Doris I'm here."

Michelle had barely touched the phone before Mr. Roberts rapped on the floor managers door 3 times and just opened the door.

"Morning Doris," Mr. Robert said while walking to a seat in her spacious office and sat down. Doris' office held a round conference table and nicely appointed office furniture. It could be described as a tidy mess of paperwork with stacks in seemingly random locations.

Doris removed her glasses, looked at Mr. Roberts and replied flatly "Good morning John".

Mr. Roberts seemed to squirm at the use of his first name but he did not argue.

Doris continued, "You remember Cathy don't you?" Cathy was a short brown haired middle-aged lady who almost seemed to blend in with the paperwork in the room.

Mr. Roberts responded curtly, "Yes, I do. Cathy has been getting paychecks here for the past 30 years, haven't you Cathy?"

Cathy seemed to just freeze and looked from Mr. Roberts to Doris.

"Cathy, why don't we just get back to this later? John has some visitors here", Doris said letting Cathy off the hook.

Mr. Roberts squirmed some more as Cathy grabbed a stack of papers and scrambled out of the room without saying a word.

Mr. Roberts flicked a microscopic dust particle off of his immaculately tailored pants and said, "Doris I need assistance with my guest here and I immediately thought of you."

Doris smiled at Mr. Roberts and said, "Imagine that." The sarcasm dripped from her lips.

Doris eyes moved from Mr. Roberts to Ed and Sasha. "How can I help you guys?"

Mr. Roberts answered "I would like for you to give them an insider's tour of the company and generally answer any questions they have so I don't have to answer them later. And if you could get them back to me before lunch that would be great."

With that he got up out of the seat and walked out the door.

Doris put her face in her hands and murmured, "I went back to school for this?"

Ed and Sasha just sat there stunned by everything that just happened. Sasha finally managed, "Is he always like that?"

Doris finally said, "Oh, he is showing off…slightly. What is it that you guys are here for?"

"Initially we were here to be mentored by Mr. Roberts and Rev. Simmons. Now I am not sure what is going on," said Ed.

"Mr. Roberts wanted us to get a view of the company so we could talk about it later," offered Sasha.

"Well that shouldn't be too difficult," said Doris. "This is just corporate America USA. It is a giant company that sucks up your life and spits out a useless pension plan after you are gone."

Doris put her face back in her hands and sighed. "I'm sorry. I am just a little extra stressed today. My daughter is sick at home and neither my husband nor I can be home to watch her because we have to work. We both have high paying jobs and spend more time working than we do seeing our family. After twenty years, you would think we would not be in the same circumstances that we started with…just with more bills."

"I am so sorry to hear about your daughter. Why don't we stay here in your office near the phone?" Sasha walked around the desk and put her hand on Doris' shoulder. "I have worked in a government building since I left college. All office buildings are the same…just different cafeteria food."

Doris lifted her head out her hands and smiled. "But isn't that food great for the first month? Then it is about as fun as watching a repeat of your favorite show for ten years straight. Why don't we grab a cup of coffee? I need to get out of this office and my daughter has my cell phone number."

"That sounds good to me. Getting out of the office is the reason why I left corporate America to begin with," said Ed.

"Great," said Doris as she grabbed some coins out of her top drawer. "Let's go."

Doris invited Michelle and Cathy along to the cafeteria for coffee. As they walked back through the maze of cubicles and hallways Ed and Sasha introduced themselves and told Doris about their backgrounds. Along the way it was obvious how the tension had cleared the air with Mr. Roberts not around. Both business and personal conversations could be heard along with the occasional burst of laughter throughout the massive office floor.

The cafeteria was just as nice as the lobby with lots of natural light through huge plate glass windows. The conversation quickly turned to the inner workings of the people in the company as they waited for their coffee to cool.

"I have been here since the company started and it was not always like this," said Cathy. "This was just a small company with less than 30 people helping pharmaceutical companies track information on their customers, the doctors and the latest research. It all changed once we went public."

Doris nodded in agreement. "I came in right before the takeover hit. John…I mean Mr. Roberts was just a sales guy when I got here. I came in to take over the Information Management team."

"I just wanted to work my nine to five and go home to spend time with my kids," Doris continued. "That was working fine but eventually the family grew and so did the bills. I decided to go back to school to get another degree so I could move up. After six years of part time classes I got a degree, a five percent pay increase, more responsibility and an education bill that I am still working to pay off."

"Are you saying that you shouldn't have gone back to school? I am considering going back," Michelle interrupted.

"No, no. It is always important to get your education," said Doris. "We did not have a company program to assist with paying for school back then so it just cost me more. I am just saying I did not get what I wanted out of it. I thought more money meant more time with my family. It actually had the opposite effect."

"Well hopefully you can rely on your kids when you retire," Cathy said. "I am going to hit retirement age in 6 months and I never married or had kids. I didn't really get into all these 401(k)s and retirement plans until 15 years ago. Even with that, my financial planner said I can only live comfortably for the next 10 years with my portfolio, pension plan and social security."

"What if I get sick or have to stay in the hospital? I don't want to rely on the government to take care of my bills. I would probably die of red tape," Cathy said despondently. "What if I live to be 80 or 90? I have several family members who are in danger of being kicked out of their homes and retirement homes because their money is running out. No one planned to live that long."

"OK…you guys are scaring me," said Michelle. "At least you have social security as a back up plan. That won't even be an option when I am ready to retire. I have been putting money in my 401K plan but the stock market keeps leap frogging around. This is the fourth job I have had since graduating 10 years ago. I was downsized and outsourced before I turned 30. You can't get a pension from a company that is not there anymore."

"I think I am going to start my own business making healthy brown bag lunches for office workers who just don't have the time to make their own and at a reasonable price," Michelle concluded with her eyes drifting off into space.

"I encourage you to do that but that is not necessarily the answer either," said Ed. "I left out of corporate America to start my own company and it has been a pure rollercoaster ride. More like a beautiful hell. It is by no means as glamorous as some people make it out to be. I am sure I will make a go of it someday but in the meantime there are lots of sleepless nights, tax forms, payrolls and personal sacrifices. I would never discourage someone from chasing their dreams but…"

"But what?" The anxiousness in Michelle's voice was obvious.

"Running your own business is like going to school where you only get graded by how much money stays in your bank account. Plus you are tested everyday where there are hundreds of right answers and thousands of wrong answers," Ed continued. "Taking a class where the right answer is given to you in a book is paramount to cheating in the entrepreneurial world. Building a company is like projecting the future. It takes a long time to get a talent like that right."

"The contracting world sits right in between running your own business and working in the corporate world," said Sasha as she sipped her mocha frappaccino. "You're a free agent so you have the freedom of being in charge of where you work and having a company structure to help take advantage of tax breaks. But at the same time the financial rug can be pulled out from under you when a project is done. No pension or two weeks notice."

"In fact, I was on a project that kept getting extended indefinitely. I was only supposed to be there for one month but it kept going for six. Then one day during an all hands staff meeting one of the employees made a suggestion about how I could work on one of the upcoming changes that was needed. The manager just said that would not work out because I would not be there at the beginning of the next month. Basically I was told I was being let go in the middle of the meeting."

"That's horrible," Doris exclaimed. "I can't believe someone would do something like that."

"You can't believe it? Most of the people in the room, many of whom were now friends, had no idea what just happened," Sasha continued. "I had to track down the manager after the meeting to make sure I understood him correctly. He just nodded and said, 'Didn't someone tell you?'"

"I don't know if I could handle being a contractor," said Michelle. "That was absolutely terrible. I don't know if I would have cried or tried to take his head off.

"Well the truth of the matter is that most companies and the government are looking to hire contractors because they can bring them on quickly and let them go at will without worrying about paying a pension," Sasha added.

The group fell quiet as they all stirred, sipped or finished off their coffee.

"At least you guys have a really nice cafeteria," said Ed trying to lighten the mood.

"Hah. If only I had a nickel for every person that ate here for the past15 years and for the next 15 years, I could retire a happy woman," said Cathy.

"Wait a minute," said Sasha. "Didn't you say Mr. Roberts used to be a sales guy here? How did he end up owning the company?"

"I heard he sold his soul to the devil," giggled Michelle.

"Close to it," said Doris. "He just outworked everyone. He never took off, was here before everyone, left after everyone and was obsessed with money…just like he is now. This is a great trait in a salesman but a terrible trait in a business owner."

"I heard he put every dime he had or could get to buy stock in the company before the IPO," added Cathy. "When the company went public he went from John the sales guy to John the near tyrant on the Board of Directors. Then it went to Mr. Roberts the complete tyrant ten years ago when he became the majority owner. I never really knew him before the company went public and I am sort of glad I didn't. You would think he was John D. Rockefeller himself."

"I hope that is not the advice he is going to give us," said Ed. "I don't want to be obsessed with money in order to be rich. How does this company function anyway?"

"We basically collect, manage, move and sell information to be blunt," answered Doris. "Whenever something is bought or sold, whether its pills, a cup of coffee or a new bank account…somebody wants to know about it. That way they can figure out how to sell that product or service again plus how to sell even more to that customer. It's all about the information."

"The internet has really messed with the company because information is easier to find and interpret. It is just so much more of it," added Cathy. "We have gone from mailing out reports in binders to shooting out reports to sales guys PDA's in real time. All in the past 7 years."

"We now have 25 offices internationally with close to 5000 employees. Some of the offices are getting ready to lose some people," said Doris.

Michelle looked at Doris in horror. "Oh no! I can't go through another downsizing."

"I don't think you have anything to worry about honey," said Cathy. "The companies' stock price is going up."

"That's a relief. After this conversation, I really don't know what I am going to do with my future," sighed Michelle.

"Well, we are here to get advice from Mr. Roberts and Rev. Simmons about getting wealthy. Maybe we will have some information to share," offered Ed.

Doris looked around as the lunch crowd started coming into the cafeteria. "It looks like it is time for you guys to get back to that advice."

Ed stopped suddenly and said, "Hey Doris...don't you guys do something with livestock?"

"Livestock? We don't deal with any animals here," she replied. "Why?"

"Um...just something about cattle," said Ed with a puzzled look on his face.

"Well...thanks for taking the time to talk to us. It was really nice to get to know all of you," said Sasha as she and Ed got up from the table.

As they walked away they could hear Michelle whisper, "Mr. Roberts is still in the building?"

There was a prompt, loud "Come in" as Ed and Sasha knocked on Mr. Roberts' office door from the stairwell. They stepped in to see Mr. Roberts standing in front of a full length mirror in a three piece suit.

"How do you like my Gordon Gecko look?" Mr. Roberts posed like a giant kid playing dress up.

Sasha walked over to Mr. Roberts to make sure his tie was properly in place. "I guess those phone calls went well?"

"Let's just say that was the best $5000 I ever lost in my life," chuckled Mr. Roberts. "It's amazing how bundles of money can cure a headache. Cuban cigar?"

"Sure...don't mind if I..." Ed saw the look on Sasha's face and quickly changed his mind. "Um, maybe later."

"Ha ha! Good answer son. Let's save that for after lunch," Mr. Roberts said as he gestured over to a table set up with hamburgers, hotdogs and all the fixings.

"I knew I smelled something good. I love bar-b-que," exclaimed Ed.

"Hotdogs are my favorites," Sasha joined in.

"What kind of capitalist doesn't like a good cookout? Help yourselves. You guys can have your martinis at a more decent hour," Mr. Roberts said as he moved over to the bar. "I promise not to have a heart attack."

The trio settled down with plates full of chicken, burgers, potato salad and hotdogs.

Mr. Roberts took a sip of his martini and asked with a grin, "So what did you guys learn today?"

Both Ed and Sasha froze in mid bite and glanced at each other. They just continued to chew slowly like the one who swallowed first would have to answer. Ed lost.

"I have a question for you. You seem to be such a really cool guy, other than the practical jokes," Ed said slowly. "But you are a completely different person with your employees. I mean they are terrified of you. What gives?"

"Ha ha! I thought you were going to choke on your burger. I guess old habits die hard," Mr. Roberts laughed. "My father was a traveling salesman and I would go with him to his office. His boss was a complete hard…uh…not a nice guy. But everyone at the office would keep coming back and work day and night to make this guy rich. I didn't get it but it works on some folks. Very well I may add too."

"My Dad passed away working for the same company and left us with no more than two dimes to rub together. I promised I would never be broke so I developed a work extremely hard and play even harder attitude."

Sasha dabbed a little potato salad from her lips and asked, "Is that why you are single now?"

"You got that right! People say that I am missing something in my life but I have come to realize that it takes different things for people to be happy. I just deeply embrace my different things. Anyone who has a problem with that can kiss my bank accounts…all six of them."

"I don't expect for anyone else to be like me and truly hope that they don't. I take full responsibility for my destiny and my actions. All wealthy people do. Only the cattle follow each other from the field to the slaughter."

"There is that cattle thing again," Ed interrupted. "What do you mean by cattle?"

"You just had coffee with them. They are the people who stay in the pasture fattening themselves on paychecks and never bothering to think they need to grow their own grass or ask 'what is the deal' with the fences around them. They just line up for retirement or financial slaughter and start shaking in their boots."

Sasha shook her head in disbelief. "These people work for you for years and you call them cattle? Don't you think you owe them something more than that?"

Mr. Roberts howled with laughter. "Are you kidding? This company pays an extra 30% of their total compensation on social security, health insurance and retirement savings. That means I pay them hundreds of thousands of dollars and then pay the government hundreds of thousands of dollars so they can give it back to them when the employee heads to the retirement slaughterhouse. They trade their time for money and then let the money slip through their hands. Whose fault is that?"

"Do you realize that Cathy has made over a million and a half dollars while she has worked here? Now I am supposed to give her some more money to keep her from dying in the slaughterhouse and she has the nerve to complain. This company held up its end of the bargain by being financially responsible. She didn't handle her financial responsibility. Off to the slaughterhouse with her!"

"You have a couple of points there but isn't that a little harsh," interjected Ed.

"Son, harsh is dying and leaving your three sons and wife with squat. I have seen harsh up close and personal. Do you know my first job ended up being to work for that hard…uh…not so nice guy? One day I really let him know how I felt about how he treated my Dad. He glared at me and didn't say a word."

Mr. Roberts stopped like he was reliving the moment.

"He reached into his desk drawer and pulled out a huge ledger. He flipped to a page and pointed to one line with my father's name on one side. He turned the old book over so I could see clearly and slid his finger from my fathers name to a total of $626,795.95. That was a ton of money back then."

"Then he asked, 'Remember the big house, beautiful furniture, wonderful vacations, your nice new clothes, the shiny new cars and big meals in the fancy restaurants?' All I could do was nod my head."

"He just slammed the book shut, told me to never be ungrateful for the money the good Lord saw fit to give me and to get the hell out of his office and go sell something."

Ed and Sasha sat silently as Mr. Roberts attempted to compose himself. Mr. Roberts leaned back slightly, breathed deeply and continued.

"Maybe that is harsh but money is the value that is given for the work you do. I learned from my great teacher and mentor that it is your responsibility to safeguard it and help it grow. Social security was designed so the country didn't have old people begging in the streets. It is not an insurance program. Then along came some guys in slick suits telling everyone to put their money in the bank or a 401K or in the stock market. Oh and by the way, don't do any work like read the small print or really try to understand what is going on with your money. Just trust them and go get a credit card."

"And don't forget to have a car note for the rest of your life and pay three times the value of a house because you don't understand compound interest, what an asset really is or how your credit score really affects your FSQ."

Sasha's head snapped up as she asked "What is an FSQ?"

"Oh that is your Financial Slave Quotient. For every day that interest is building on your house, car, education, credit cards or whatever and you do not have an asset to balance it out is a day that you HAVE to work."

"As in you can't visit a dying family member or take care of mommy dearest because you OWE money and you HAVE to work. Most people are on track to die financial slaves. Its like they never ever got a dime a day in their lives."

"If they are poor, they are slaves to the stuff they wasted their money on. If they are middle-class, they are slaves to the bills they accumulated."

"Financial slaves…that is pretty deep," said Ed.

Mr. Roberts nodded and continued, "You see indentured servants worked for a period of time to pay off their debt and then they were free. Financial slaves have no way to catch up with their debts because the debts keep growing everyday and their wages barely keep up with inflation. And the cattle keep slavin' away."

Sasha asked, "Do you ever feel guilty about having so much money while knowing so many are financial slaves?"

Mr. Roberts looked at Sasha and just chuckled. "You have some kooky notions there little lady. It takes discipline and study to be financially free. I can't make anybody do what they are supposed to do. And my money doesn't live in a bubble. When I blow $5000 in Vegas, everyone who works there gets a chance to save their financial souls with a new paycheck. My $3000 Gordon Gekko suit takes care of the tailor, the cloth makers and needle makers. I just make sure that I always, always, always have more money coming in than going out."

"I have never heard anyone say financial soul," said Sasha. "That's an interesting concept."

"That's not a concept. That is what everyone has and they can trade it for a few knick knacks they will forget about in a week or they can use it for its real use. To be free, secure and have the time that God gave you to enjoy."

"But that is the Reverends department," Mr. Roberts said as he took the last bite of a hotdog. "I just kick ass and have a kick ass time. Speaking of which, it is time that I go kick some. You guys are going to be on the Rev's turf tomorrow."

Chapter 3

The Information Age Lifestyle

Tuesday morning's 20th floor had a different look. As Ed and Sasha stepped off of the elevator, there was no crunch of dust underfoot and the junk was all but gone from the floor and yet it was eerily silent. Now they got a sense of how large the place was with the morning light shining from one end of the massive floor to the other.

"Looks like brand new, huh?"

Ed didn't jump this time but he flinched as Rev. Simmons rolled up next to them with his janitor's cart.

"Do you guys ever quit?" Ed didn't bother turning around just so he did not look like the village clown again.

"Why bother? Got to keep you youngsters on your toes," the Reverend said smiling.

"Good morning Rev. Simmons. It is nice to get a welcoming committee today," Sasha said cheerily.

"So Mr. Roberts must have got you with possum yesterday. I keep telling him he needs to step his game up," Rev. Simmons sighed. "Oh well, let's get rolling."

The Reverend turned the cart and started walking towards the janitor's closet. The clicks of Ed and Sasha's heels could be heard with the light whine of one of the cart's wheels.

Ed asked, "How was your weekend?"

The Reverend half turned to them beaming as he kept up his quick pace. "Absolutely marvelous. I 'coptered over to the children and the grand kids and we took the yacht over to my neighbor's island. They were renewing their vows. It was a real tear jerker. They are some of the nicest people you will ever meet."

"You took a helicopter to a yacht to an island? That is incredible," Sasha exclaimed. "You don't seem like the yachting type."

"I'm not. I would much rather fly the chopper but the grand kids love the water," the Reverend explained as they walked into the closet.

Looking inside for the first time, Ed and Sasha realized that the closet was actually the same size as the front room to Mr. Roberts' office. The janitor's equipment in this room looked like it had seen some use. There was the same non-descript door on the side of this room too.

"So you have an office like Mr. Roberts too?" Sasha was bursting to see what was in the room.

"We have completely different taste," Rev. Simmons replied. "Take a look."

Ed and Sasha stepped into what looked like someone's house. The hardwood floors gleamed in the sunlight beaming through the bright windows. Furniture sat arranged in cozy settings to welcome guest in for relaxing conversations. The windows facing the east were made of stained glass and gave a reverent glow to an eating area sitting next to a full kitchen.

"Oh man…I mean oh man! This is…I mean wow," Ed managed to say.

Sasha walked over to the wall next to the library of books that went to the ceiling. She stood in front of framed pictures of children's drawings that covered every inch of the wall from left to right and floor to ceiling. She covered her mouth with her hands and just stared.

"This is so beautiful. Are these from your children? I could never imagine…" Sasha seemed on the verge of tears.

Ed walked over and wrapped his arms around her. Rev. Simmons stood next to them. No words were spoken as they took in the imagination of children.

"These are from our children, grandchildren, nephews, nieces, family friend's children …" Rev. Simmons looked in awe of the pictures as if he were seeing them for the first time too. "This is my wife's room. She collected these pieces over the years and designed this room around them."

"I have to meet her. To do this is part love and part genius. I can just feel her in here," said Sasha.

"She passed away 13 years ago, a few years after we finished this building and this room. She put herself and everything she loved in this room," the Reverend said. "It is truly amazing what the human spirit can do given enough time and freedom."

Rev. Simmons looked at the young couple staring at the pictures. "Let me guess…you guys want to get married and start a family but financial considerations are slowing you down," said the Reverend.

"Yeah, something like that," Ed replied with a sniff.

Let's sit down and talk about what you guys have learned so far," said Rev. Simmons as he walked over to an oversized lounge chair. Ed and Sasha sat in the love seat across from him.

"We were talking about that last night," replied Ed. "Basically it seems that in the end it does not matter how much money you make, it is all in how you take care of it. It is your responsibility to take care of your finances and no one else's."

"And not to wait on the government or rely on other peoples advice without knowing exactly what they are talking about. He started talking about saving the financial soul but said that was your territory" added Sasha.

Rev. Simmons leaned in and asked, "So this leads up to…?"

"I don't think we are exactly sure," volunteered Ed.

Rev. Simmons lit up. "Perfect! I didn't want Mr. Roberts to steal all of my thunder. I suppose he told you about the cattle thing too?"

Sasha looked shocked. "You don't agree with him do you?"

"Not whole heartedly. But it is what it is. The proof is in the assets, cash flow and bank accounts," Rev. Simmons said while standing up. "Let's get moving to today's lessons."

"Race you to the 35th floor," Rev. Simmons yelled as he ran to the door next to the kitchen and took off up the stairwell.

Ed looked at Sasha and muttered, "Not again" and chased her through the door and up the steps.

Rev. Simmons calmly sat crossed legged on the landing of the 35th floor stairwell humming lightly with his eyes closed as Sasha and Ed caught up to him.

"Let me guess," said Ed trying to catch his breath. "You are a millionaire janitor and magical Buddhist too."

"Nope," replied Rev. Simmons as he opened one eye to look at them. "I am a multi-millionaire janitor. The magical Buddhist part is just to make you youngin's look bad."

The Reverend popped up and walked through the door urging his two companions along. The 35th floor had a completely different feel to the 29th floor. There were no cubicles but there were large plants, desk, chairs and sofas laid out like dozens of people bought their home offices in with them.

Suddenly there was a loud "Eeeeee" as a woman ran down the hallway with her arms wide open to hug the Reverend. Behind her was another little "Eeeeee" as a five year old raced behind her to hug the Reverend's knee.

The Reverend warmly embraced her and scooped up the child. "Good morning Sarah. Good morning Bobby." Mr. Roberts looked like a doting grandfather as he tickled the little boy's stomach.

Calls of "good morning Rev. Simmons", "the Reverend is here" and "hey Reverend", came from all directions as a dozen people walked out to greet him.

"Good morning everyone," the Reverend responded heartily. "Say hello to my friends Sasha and Ed." Ed and Sasha were immediately swarmed with hugs, hand shakes and pats on the back. The people wore relaxed clothes with a few khakis and polo shirts thrown in. They ranged from the early twenties to late seventies. Every one of them smiled and looked like they enjoyed being in the office.

"This is nothing like Mr. Roberts' office set up," Ed commented. "If I worked in an office like this I would have never left the corporate world."

"Aaahh but that is the catch," replied Rev. Simmons. "This is not the corporate world. Each person here owns their own business. They run a cooperative to lease this space…lease to own of course…and use it to be near each other for convenience and encouragement."

Sasha looked puzzled. "What is it that everyone does?"

Rev. Simmons let Bobby down and asked Sarah to fill them in.

Sarah smiled and said, "We are a cooperative of small businesses that are on a mission to create financial education schools all across the country. We have accountants, teachers, real estate agents, insurance agents, finance managers, mortgage lenders…"

"And don't forget ministers," interjected Rev. Simmons.

"Oh yes, and of course ministers. In many ways this is a financial education ministry. Over 60% of people in this country are in financial slavery. Most of them will never see a real retirement or will remain financially enslaved for their entire lives," she continued.

"It really does not have to be that way. Everyone goes to school to learn how to get a job to make money but they never learn how to manage that money. Then after years of work, they realize that hundreds of thousands of dollars seemed to have just disappeared. But more importantly, their time, joy and freedom to be with family have disappeared too.

"We want to give everyone the opportunity to have a continuous financial education. In fact, classes are held every Saturday," said Sarah.

"That is a great idea. But do you think people will want to come out every Saturday? Some people don't want to obsess over money," Sasha inquired.

Rev. Simmons put his hand on Sasha's shoulder and smiled. "What do you think they are doing anyway? If you wake up at 6:00am to be to work by 8:00 and then don't get home until 6:30pm and don't unwind until 7:30 just so you can do that all over again…don't you think that is obsessive."

"And if you don't have anything to show for all of your time except stuff and more bills, then it is completely useless and absolutely insane," agreed Sarah as she picked up Bobby and gave him a kiss on his cheek. "I lost three years of my time with my son for a new car I could not afford. He is worth more than leather seats and a shiny logo on bad credit."

"Your financial education has to be ongoing. It is not about reading a book, cutting up your credit cards and being back in debt two years later," Sarah continued. "Tax laws, income vehicles, interest rates, financing rules and the money world changes constantly. You need to be in an environment where like minded people are learning together. Becoming wealthy is a lifestyle and learning with others is where it all starts."

"In fact," said Sarah as she put down Bobby and grabbed his hand, "Here comes proof now."

The elevator doors opened and a large group of people stepped off. On seeing the Reverend the hugs and hand shakes started again as Rev. Simmons introduced Ed and Sasha once more.

After the greetings the Reverend asked the group, "How was the field trip guys?"

"I have been in the real estate business for years and I did not know so much about the mortgage side. Ralph really laid it out for us," replied an older short gentleman wearing a fisherman's hat.

"Heck," replied Ralph. "If I went in and bought that house without Sal's advice I would have lost my shirt."

The group agreed with each person reporting on what they did not know and how the house they just finished looking at could have ruined them.

The Reverend asked, "How many of you would have bought that house as an investment property before today?"

Eight of the ten people raised their hands.

"How many people would buy that property now?"

Not one hand went up.

"We were explaining to Ed and Sasha here how important it is to learn about wealth in groups," said Sarah.

A chorus of "Oh yes" and "Definitely" rang out.

A middle-aged woman with long gray hair spoke up. "I had been in debt for my entire life. That is all I ever saw growing up. My parents always worked and I barely saw them. Sometimes they had two jobs at a time and I never once heard them talking about money other than to argue about spending it.

"I swore I would never be like them so I went to college, got a good job, and married a man with a good job. The next thing you know both of us are working all the time and had no time for the kids. I became my parents...just with more money."

"I never thought of it that way. Come to think of it, I don't think I know of anyone who doesn't have to work constantly to get by," said Ed.

"Exactly Sugar," the lady continued. "It was not until I met the Reverend and started meeting with these folks that things started to change. Just realizing that I was not the only one struggling with financial mis-education helped. I see money differently now. It does not control me, I control it."

The Reverend added, "You must...absolutely have to...and can not possibly gain wealth without understanding money. Knowledge of finances is more important than your job or that "job" education. Lottery winners are usually broke in 3 years. Wage earners usually stay broke for a lifetime."

"Amen Rev. Simmons", came out from the crowd.

"I know you guys have some more analyzing of your property field trip to do so we won't hold you up," said Rev. Simmons as he turned to Sarah. "Sarah could you and Bobby show them around while I get lunch prepared."

Bobby hopped around gleefully. "Can I show them the game, mommy?"

"OK, but remember the rules," she said sternly.

Bobby grabbed Ed's hand and started pulling him down the hall.

"It looks like you have a new friend," Sasha laughed. Bobby took off dragging Ed helplessly behind him. Sasha and Sarah started chatting.

"We want to start a family soon too," Sasha said as they strolled down the hall.

"Well you guys are starting off right. I was not kidding when I said I missed three years of Bobby's life. I can't get that time back," Sarah said solemnly. "I remember when a $25,000 job meant a lot in college and I could manage just fine. Then I moved up to $60,000 once I got into my career. When I got over $100,000, my husband and I thought we had everything together to start a family."

"Every time our income went up our expenses went up. Add a newborn into the mix and we just went overboard. Name brand clothes, tons of toys, not to mention the diaper and formula basics. I even bought a luxury station wagon. I could see myself taking Bobby and his little toddler friends on trips..."

Sarah's eyes glazed over as she continued, "Then the bills kept coming, the money arguments with Bobby's daddy got louder and the office hours got longer. My husband and I had to work harder to keep up the lifestyle that we wanted for the baby. And all the baby wanted was us. When I got home late one evening and heard Bobby call the baby sitter 'Mommy' I just broke down. At the same time my husband and I fell apart."

"Look," Sarah said stopping suddenly. "Promise me you guys will care for the money you have now and not gamble your future on the money you think you will make. I got Bobby back in my life. I am not sure how or if I can get my husband back."

"Oh Sarah!" Sasha looked her in the eyes. "I am so sorry to hear that. I promise. You have my word on it."

Sarah wiped at her eye before a tear could form. "Good," she said smiling again. "You guys look so cute together."

As they rounded the corner, they saw Ed sitting in the midst of 10 children playing together over 2 board games. Ed stood up and walked over to the ladies as they approached. Bobby didn't even look up.

"Baby," Ed said looking at Sasha. "These kids are going over assets and liabilities on a board game. I had to get out of there before they made me look silly."

Sarah nodded and said, "That's right. None of our kids are going to get stuck in the same trap we or our parents did. Actually, they have less choice than we do. Pensions, jobs for life, social security and the other things we grew up knowing will soon virtually be non-existent. If they aren't financially literate, they simply will not make it."

"That is so true," Sasha agreed. "There are already some jobs you can't get without having good credit and soon other things like car insurance are going to be added to that."

"Well we plan to have financial education schools for people of all ages," continued Sarah. "Everyone deals with money every day whether they want to or not. It is even a national security issue."

"I never heard that one," Ed said.

"Think about it," said Sarah. "If the majority of the country is financially illiterate, then bankruptcies, foreclosures and massive credit card debt will be rampant. Imagine if a state had hundreds of foreclosures at the same time. That tax base is wiped out plus those same people are going to need public services to get their lives back together. That means more taxes are needed. And if these people do not get a financial education, they will get into the exact same financial mess again and give that mentality to their children."

"I think that is already happening," Sasha said while looking at the children focused on their game.

"Exactly," continued Sarah. "And we already know that when people struggle financially all sorts of social ills pop up. The crime rate goes up and the community structure goes down. Parents work harder and the children fall behind. We don't have to wait for an attack from another country. We will suffer from our own financial cancer.

"In the mean time, here we have a community structure to allow people to learn about their own finances. Plus we partnered with a separate group of professionals who work with the individual and couples privately to help manage their debt and repair their credit. These guys can also give financial advice on real estate, investing and even buying a car."

"I wish we heard about this awhile ago. Right now we could use all the help we can get." Ed said.

"Of course, there is more to learn about what we are doing but I think the Reverend is ready for lunch with you guys and he can give you the details," Sarah said. "His deserts are to die for."

Chapter 4

The Financial Knowledge Age

Back in Rev. Simmons office, Ed and Sasha were welcomed in by the Reverend who did not have his customary blue janitors' uniform. He seemed very relaxed in his jeans and plaid shirt. "Please, please have a seat. I was just getting everything finished up here," he said while directing them toward the kitchen area. The light shining through the stained glass windows reflected brightly off the pots and pans hanging above the kitchen island and the stainless steel appliances.

As they took their seats on the island barstools facing the kitchen Sasha asked, "What made you and your wife decide to add a living area into an office building?"

"We always knew it was just as important to take care of our mental and physical well being as well as the financial. We lived here during most of the finishing stages of construction." Rev. Simmons had a light chuckle while reflecting. "The night before one of the city inspectors came through we were up all night installing 500 fluorescent lights so we could get the go ahead to finish construction. We were so grateful to have a place to relax right here in the building?"

Ed asked curiously, "But why do you and Mr. Roberts stay in rooms behind fake janitors closets?"

"He wants to keep the knives out of his back", the Reverend muttered real low while chopping salad.

"What did you say?" Sasha leaned in to hear him better.

"Oh nothing," said Rev. Simmons speaking louder. "I just said he has his reasons. He will tell you when the time comes."

"I stay here because it reminds me of what I was doing when I first started. I am not a business man per se. I started as a janitor after dropping out of high school to take care of my sisters when my mother passed. I happened to befriend a great teacher who taught me the secret of money and mentored me to financial success. That is why I mentor now."

Ed leaned in with Sasha to hear well. "Wait, what do you mean the secret of money?"

"Compound interests my friends. The Romans hated it so much they tried to get rid of it completely from their monetary system. Einstein said it was the greatest force in the universe," Rev. Simmons replied. "If you owe money then you are on the losing side of compound interests and it is merciless. If you are the one the money is coming to, then you will quickly become very wealthy."

Sasha sat back with a puzzled look on her face. "That makes sense but why isn't that something we learned in school?"

"Unfortunately, societal education teaches people to face the wrong way when it comes to money. Schools are more focused on teaching students how to get jobs and get money. There is very little to no education on how to the keep money," the Reverend replied.

"It really makes no sense that 60% of Americans are in a financial mess. But then you realize that all of the great education we have received is nearly 100% focused on working for a living. Continuing financial education is nearly unheard of in our public school systems.

Sasha sipped on the sweet tea Rev. Simmons served them and pondered what he was saying. "You said that these are not how to lessons but why lessons. So why do so many people have so many problems with money?"

Without hesitation the Reverend smiled broadly and said, "Fear! If you had no idea about how to gain wealth other than work for 40 years, then you would not have a great impression of money. Without continuing financial education you can not possibly keep up with new tax laws, real estate, banking, investing or saving. You are scared of most that which you do not understand. It seems that money and raising children are the two things people assume you are just supposed to know about yet they are often the two things people are most confused about.

"That is why so many kids are turned off by education and working. All they see is their parents working hard, complaining about not having enough money and not having any time to enjoy themselves. Who wants to get stuck in that rut?"

"I am constantly reading books and looking at financial TV shows but I think I still fall into the scared group," Ed said quietly.

"If your surgeon said he constantly read books and looked at the doctor shows on TV but never worked with other medical professionals or studied with his peers, would you let him start cutting away on you", replied the Reverend.

"I think I get your point," nodded Ed.

"Don't take it the wrong way. You are not the only one. Millions of people have gone through their entire lives looking for the big payday even though they were getting paid everyday.

"Money is a belief system. You are born into the Church of Money whether you want to be or not. Even homeless people are in the church because you have to have a means of exchanging value to get the food or shelter needed.

"The Church of Money changes rituals and philosophies without informing all of its followers. The rituals of 401K, the 30 year mortgage, social security, stock market investing and savings plans are being rewritten as we speak. If you are not a devout disciple of money, then you are a true heathen and the church offers very little mercy.

"Belief is the essentially the way you 'be living'. People will say they believe in certain things but the way they live obviously point in the opposite direction. An easy example is the drug dealer who wears a diamond crucifix, claims he believes in Jesus but lives 95% of his life in un-Christ like ways.

"A more subtle and more devious example is the parent who believes that their child is the most important thing to them in the world yet HAVE to spend more time at work than with their child. Not being able to take off from work to take care of a sick child or ailing family member because you OWE money is moral neglect. The vast majority of the time, this is not because of a lack of money but a simple lack of financial education.

"I guess money is a belief system", said Ed as Rev. Simmons refilled his glass of tea. "Many religions have issues with money. You know…the money being the root of all evil thing."

"The root of all evil is not money", said Rev. Simmons. "If it was, the church would not ask for 10% of it. Who wants 10% of evil? Ignorance of money is the root of a lot of evil. Most crimes are a result of financial ignorance. The money was embezzled because the banker did not manage her own money correctly. The merchandise was stolen because the store clerk did not know of any other way to get the money.

"Wealthy people rarely end up in prison...not because they are so smart but because they have no real reason to steal. They have what the criminals ultimately want...freedom. True wealth is when going to work is an option...not mandatory for not being thrown into the street."

A loud ding sent Rev. Simmons springing over to the oven. "I love cooking now. I used to hate it but it is one of those small ways you can save money instead of going out plus it brings people closer together. Especially a young couple," he said winking at Ed and Sasha.

Sasha sniffed and commented, "That smells great. I guess that makes you a janitor and a cook. How did you become a multi-millionaire?"

"I always follow the secret of business which is to care for people", replied the Reverend as he grabbed for the oven mitts.

"That's it? That seems pretty simple to be a secret", Ed said with a confused look on his face.

"Most secrets are", answered Rev. Simmons. It must be a secret if 85% of startups go out of business in five years. Compound interests is a simple secret that stares homeowners, car buyers and credit card users right in the face...yet they don't understand what it is. Even when that compound interest has its boot on their throat.

"A successful business man always cares for people and by transference he cares for what they care about. Whether it is the quality, service or price for his customers or the welfare of the people he works with. That has to be first in every aspect of the business...even the part the customer doesn't see.

"I am not an expert in running a church, a chain of restaurants, real estate development or network marketing but I care about the people that come in contact with my businesses. Therefore I care about the people I hire to run these companies. I only work with the best people I can find and I share the wealth. People are the ones with the money who are or may become your customers. Human Relations is your biggest cost in business so you had better care for your employees and contractors. That is exactly like caring for your money.

"This business secret applies to all businesses period", concluded the Reverend as he turned around with flourish holding two plates with cheese steak calzones, seasoned crispy French fries and a chopped salad. "I bought these calzones from the grand kids for their school fund raisers. The cutest sales people I have ever seen. I think I have six boxes left."

"I don't understand how Mr. Roberts can be so successful when he treats his people so horribly", Sasha said shaking her head.

Rev. Simmons finished chewing his fries and said, "Don't confuse management style for caring. His people stay with him because he has the best health benefits around and he has implemented profit sharing so his employees can share in the success of the company. He may not be the cuddliest guy but his people have had a job to go to everyday, a paycheck that arrives on time and his customers and stockholders are all pleased. He may not be first on some of his employees Christmas list but at least they can have a list to begin with.

"However he is an industrial age manager facing information age issues. The reason why the 20th floor is empty is because the print and mail shops used to be down here. E-mail and the internet made paper reports almost obsolete for his customers so those functions got removed or outsourced.

"When we were young, getting a job that allowed you to get a company pension and medical benefits was the thing to do. Now that is obsolete. We also moved around less and had job security through seniority. Now the longer you stay, the more it cost to keep you after raises so it now could be the first hired is the first fired.

"Some of the things that John did to stay in business are starting to work against him. Whole industries have been shaken by technology and the internet. Many are just starting to recover and others have simply disappeared. John has seen this coming for awhile. He has gotten more and more upset that he can not protect his people the way he used to and the frustrations just show up sometimes.

"Oh. I guess I never looked at it that way", said Sasha. "But don't you feel that same pressure with your businesses?"

"John and I are just different beast", replied the Reverend. "I chose to take time for a wife and family. He chose to work hard all the time. Now he is ready to get out and enjoy the spoils of his hard work his way. For me, I look forward to helping people gain wealth in the Financial Knowledge Age."

"Hey, hey…come on", Ed interrupted. "I just got used to the Information Age. Now we have a new one?"

"The Financial Knowledge Age is a subset of the Information Age. You see, the Information Age gave us the ability to communicate and access information easily and instantaneously world wide. As a result, the value of information has dropped tremendously. Outsourcing occurs when it is cheaper for someone to access information over there than it is over here. Presto…your job is at risk.

"This means the individual has more responsibility than ever to protect themselves from economic hardships. The smart investor who studies investing continuously is going to have a stronger portfolio for retirement than the guy who doesn't. The person with more knowledge of the real estate market will quickly outpace the person who prefers to channel surf and wait for Aunt Susie to pass.

Sasha thought about that quietly and then asked, "Well what about my 401(k) plan? That takes care of my retirement right?"

"Unfortunately it will not, unless you are an executive making $150,000 a month or more. That is who the 401(k) was designed for so they could save a few more dollars The 401(k) will not work for 80% of Americans. What your parents had was a Defined Benefits Plan which is a true pension that covers you for life until you die. A Defined Contribution Plan or 401(k) is a savings plan that only covers you until it runs out.

"Also remember your 401k plan is subject to market fluctuations. So what happens if the market is in recession when it is time for you to withdraw funds? After the baby boomers suck up social security and then live longer, what happens to the next generation of retirees?

"The government does not have the financial capacity to save you. If 75 million of the coming baby boomer retirees received just $1000 per month then that is $75 billion per month. That would be like Katrina hit every month. Even if only 10 million got the $1000 per month that would still be $120 billion each year. Of course, that would be over $1 trillion in 10 years."

"Oh, I think I am going to have a headache", Sasha sighed sounding exhausted.

"The key to being wealthy is to know what you are doing. You can't solve your financial problems with the same thinking. Wealthy simply means being financially intelligent. Being poor simply means being financially unintelligent.

"What being computer illiterate meant in the Information Age is what being financially illiterate will mean in the Financial Knowledge Age. And it won't be just the poor who will have problems. The Church of Money has no mercy on anyone who does not study at her feet so the middle class and upper class can hit the bricks just as well."

The Reverends words hung in the air as he took a bite out of his calzone. Ed and Sasha sat in silence finishing off the salad and sipping tea.

"I don't know if I feel better or worse about all of this", said Sasha. What can I do to help people like Doris, Cathy and Michelle? They seem to be stuck in a financial black hole."

"You have a good heart Sasha", replied the Reverend. "You can simply encourage them to study their money. If they are serious about it then join with them and learn as much as you can together. It is when groups of people study that great things are accomplished."

Rev. Simmons stood up, walked around the island, stood in front of Sasha and put both hands on her shoulders. "I also want you to know something that many people know to be true but don't want to think about." He cleared his throat and looked in her eyes. "There will always be wealthy people and there will always be poor people and there is nothing you can do about that but decide what side you want to live on. If you want to help poor people…don't be one of them."

He let her go and walked back over to the split oven and looked at the timer on the lower door. "Five minutes," he said to himself. Then he turned back to Ed and Sasha and continued, "Poverty occurs in a wide array of circumstances. Creating wealth takes energy and you should not be ashamed of expending that energy or enjoying its fruits."

"Financial winners are willing to study more, want more control and invest for higher returns. Financial losers do not invest at all and expect their family, the company they work for or the government to take care of them when they can't work anymore.

"And ultimately what we all want is to be happy with the time we have here on earth. Money does not guarantee that. Some people have the ability to enjoy themselves no matter what the circumstances. They are the wealthiest of all people. Yet monetary wealth allows great things to occur. From the very building we are in to works of art to kindergarten classes to…well you get the picture.

"You guys have really put it on us. This is a lot to absorb", Ed said shaking his head.

Rev. Simmons smiled as the oven timer went off. "You guys have a few more days with us so don't fret. But in the meantime, you get to feast on the Simmons' Grandkids Special." The Reverend pulled three hot apple tarts from the oven and slid them unto a large plate. Then he grabbed vanilla ice cream from the freezer and scooped generous portions onto each tart.

The ice cream instantly started melting all over the tarts as he sat the plate in the middle of the island. The Reverend handed a spoon to Ed and Sasha said, "The rules are that whatever cream and tart is left on the plate after you finish yours is fair game. Alright...go!"

Ed rushed in with his spoon shoving part ice cream and hot apple tart into his mouth and immediately regretted it. He jumped off the barstool with his mouth open yelping, "Aaargh! Hot and good, Hot and good."

Sasha and the Reverend just laughed as Ed fanned his mouth with his hand. "It may take one of us longer to learn", Sasha said.

After finishing the desert which tasted much better when cooled, Ed and Sasha prepared to leave. The Reverend asked as they walked toward the door, "Are either of you guys afraid of heights?"

Both Ed and Sasha shook their heads no. "Then we are all set for a great field trip. Just ride up to the top floor and take the stairs to the roof when you come in tomorrow", Rev. Simmons said.

As the couple left the Reverend and headed for the elevator, Ed mumbled with his mouth still tingling, "You never know what to expect from these guys."

Chapter 5

Bird's Eye Real Estate

On Wednesday Ed and Sasha rode the elevator directly up to the top floor and took the steps up to the roof like Rev. Simmons told them. As they opened the door and their eyes adjusted to the bright morning light a voice jumped at them from around the corner.

"Congratulations you old…oh crap. It's you guys," said a visibly disappointed Mr. Roberts.

"I guess I should be used to all of this by now but I have never had to…" Sasha stopped in mid-sentence. Her eyes moved from the sign in front of them to the helicopter right behind it.

"Yes it is a beautiful sight isn't it," said Mr. Roberts glowing. He nearly skipped across the roof top and took the white handkerchief out of his brilliantly white suit jacket and pretended to buff the large white sign with red letters saying 'Congratulations! It's a Billionaire'.

The white helicopter sitting behind the sign was the largest Ed or Sasha had ever seen. Mr. Roberts came back over, slid in between them and gave them both a squeeze. "Maybe one day we can grow up to be like him", he said gleefully.

"Be yourself and you'll do just fine," Rev. Simmons said loudly from behind them.

This time Mr. Roberts jumped, finally giving Ed and Sasha something to laugh at. Mr. Roberts spun around and picked the Reverend up with a bear hug. "I knew you would do it", he said exuberantly.

Mr. Roberts grabbed Rev. Simmons hand and stuck it out like they were doing the waltz while singing "You'll never find…a billionaire like mine", in every off key imaginable.

"Thanks John", the Reverend gasped as his feet dangled in the air.

Sasha ran over and gave Rev. Simmons a hug. "You're a billionaire? That is amazing. Why didn't you tell us?"

"Oh wow, oh wow! Can I touch you?" Ed smiled as he shook the Reverend's hand and hugged him. Rev. Simmons had added a sports jacket to his jeans and plaid shirt combination.

"It really is just a number", Rev. Simmons said calmly. "Thirty years from now a millionaire will be middle class. Just like a movie with popcorn used to cost 20 cents. Heck, you can't even find a cent button on a keyboard. I just got to a billion quicker. I really do appreciate all of this though."

"As a heathen to a minister, your modesty makes me want to puke," Mr. Roberts said rolling his eyes. "Let's get over to the club and get this party started right."

"Sure but what is that?" The Reverend pointed to the white helicopter that gleamed majestically in the sunlight.

"Look buddy", Mr. Roberts said as he wrapped his massive arm around the Reverends shoulder and looked at the helicopter. "I know you well enough to remember how you would look at all the big helicopters in your magazines. I also know you well enough to know that you would have to be pulled kicking and screaming into it before you realized how nice it would be to have one of your own. Just like the big house, just like the island and just like your first helicopter."

"It would be nice to be able to carry more of the kids...", the Reverend thought out loud.

"Yeah, yeah whatever", said Mr. Roberts as he walked to the helicopter. "Just get in before you ask how much it cost. You kids hop in the back. I only leased this puppy for one day."

Everyone settled into the leather upholstered seats as the Reverend expertly flipped switches, ran checks and put on a white helmet that looked like something out of a sci-fi military movie.

"This bird here is a beaut", the Reverend cooed as the powerful engines gently lifted the group off the rooftop. "Let's take the long tour".

The helicopter swiftly moved from the building and arched left quickly leaving the office park behind. After flying over parks, roads and bridges, Mr. Roberts and Rev. Simmons started pointing out the windows at the residential houses on the ground like little kids and saying "Mine and that one too...I saw that one first...".

Over the dull roar of the engine above them Sasha inquired loudly, "What are you guys talking about?"

Mr. Roberts turned the passenger seat around with ease to face them in the back seats. "Between the two of us we have several hundred residential and commercial properties. That is one of the ways we came into the millionaires realm. Of course, we learned some very painful lessons with that."

"Extremely painful", Rev. Simmons added from the front.

"Real estate is one of the best ways to grow your fortune but just like any business it has its perils", continued Mr. Roberts. "And when you are talking about hundreds of thousands to several millions of dollars at time, it can get scary quickly."

"I think these guys can handle it, said the Reverend. "What is the secret of money?"

"Compound interest", replied Ed.

"Great", Rev. Simmons enthused. "What is the secret of business?"

"Care about people," Sasha answered quickly.

"Gees Rev," said Mr. Roberts. "Are you going to give away all of our secrets?"

The Reverend replied, "What? Are you saving them for your kids? What good is talking about real estate or any other business without the secrets?"

"Well you don't have to get personal", Mr. Roberts grinned. "Then how about this one? What is your largest personal expense?"

"Your house", Ed offered.

"That's one point off of your scoreboard son", Mr. Roberts said. "Your largest expense in life is taxes. From those extras pennies for the Snickers Bar you bought when you were nine to the first time you got your paycheck and asked 'who is FICA', taxes have been in your life.

"The government likes it when you buy and develop real estate. It creates places to live, eat, work and of course generates more taxes by helping the economy in general. Many of the most favorable tax laws work for real estate investors. Real estate investing also offers the largest growth opportunities for your wealth and is a superior investment over stocks, bonds and mutual funds. "

Sasha let this sink in while she stared down at green and asphalt patches below. "What about all the risk that is involved in real estate?"

"There is risk in every money making opportunity but there are many measures including insurance to safe guard against losses. Another way to think about it is to realize that just about every time you ever went to sleep in your life has been on someone's property. Someone took the risk at some point to own the property and somewhere along the line someone else paid for the privilege of being there."

"Real estate investing has always seemed so complicated to me", Ed said to no one in particular.

"So is running a business or a computer. When I first got in a helicopter I had no idea where the on button was", Rev. Simmons said from the front. "But that is where study, experience and team work comes in. You prepare and at some point you just do it."

"Once you study enough to know what kind of real estate deals you want to do then you look at assembling a team of professionals to help and advice you", Mr. Roberts added.
I work with real estate lenders, escrow officers, appraiser, home inspector, real estate attorney, bookkeeper, real estate accountant, tax accountant,

insurance agent and property managers. I also keep a list of folks like a handyman, cleaning service, landscaper, roofer and plumber as contractors. The point is to use professionals. Saving money by trying to do it all yourself is for the extremely foolish.

"Once you get into real estate, the thing you realize is that it doesn't take special genius or a pile of cash to get started. Plus once you get into the real estate world, you will find people willing to mentor you and develop long term relationships. You can simply go to local real estate seminars, real estate clubs or to a community college's real estate classes to locate mentors.

"Just start small in a location close to you in an area of town you are familiar with, create a winning formula by investing in one area of real estate like small houses to gain experience and keep reading to fill the most valuable real estate of all which is between your ears", Mr. Roberts concluded.

"Sweet memories below", Rev. Simmons yelled pointing to a bunch of row houses.

Mr. Roberts reached over and gave the Reverend's shoulder a squeeze. "We never could have imagined 45 years ago that we would fly over the old neighborhood in a helicopter on your billionaire day."

Turning back to Ed and Sasha Mr. Roberts said, "Down there was our training ground. We bought the brownstone on the end together. The Rev and his wife stayed in the basement apartment and I used the top level to entertain guest and have sales meetings. Sweet memories indeed but I much prefer the present."

Mr. Roberts' voice trailed off as the helicopter hovered over the two old friend's stomping grounds. Riding in a helicopter gave Ed and Sasha a completely different perspective on the power of real estate.

Ed wondered out loud. "So someone owns every square foot of land down there?"

"Yes sir," Mr. Roberts replied. "Well mostly they do with a banks help but that is the secret of real estate...leverage. You can borrow from a bank 80% of the cost of an investment, while you put up the remaining 20% of your money. With $40,000 you can borrow $160,000 from a bank for a $200,000 rental property. Even if you just break even with rental income and your expenses, in seven years the property could appreciate 5% a year to $281,000. Your equity which is the $281,000 minus what you owe the bank is now $101,420.

"Compare that to putting $40,000 in a mutual fund. During those same seven years, if it earns 5%, it could give you a whopping $14,000. Now which one of you kids wants the $101,420?"

Ed and Sasha playfully put their hands in the air and shouted, "Me, me. I want it!"

Mr. Roberts grinned and leaned in closer to them. "It gets even better. This is how the real money is made. Invest $40,000 and borrow $160,000 from the bank for a rental property. Remember the property could appreciate 5% per year which means you can borrow out the appreciation every two years and invest in a new property with 10% down. After seven years you can have four properties worth $2,022,218 and your net equity will be $273,198. Now who wants $273,198 in seven years?"

Ed would have jumped out of his seat trying to raise his hand if the seatbelt didn't hold him down.

"Calm down son", Mr. Roberts continued. "All you do is invest in a property, get the original investment back, keep control of the original property, move the money into a new property, get the investment back and just repeat the process."

"Now of course that is a simplistic overview. You have to really know what you are doing with a solid and continuing real estate education and sound advice.

If one of the properties ends up being a bad investment or a rental property stays vacant, then you are overleveraged and things can get painful."

"Extremely painful", Rev. Simmons added again from the front.

"So you can put 20% down and get 100% ownership in the property plus 100% of the appreciation and 100% of the deductions while the bank lets you borrow 80% of the money," said Mr. Roberts.

"And remember the banks want you to borrow the money because that is how they make money. Plus since you would create a business entity to control your investments, you can hold a property for a minimum of one year and get a capital gains tax rate of around 15% which is lower than the rate of around 33% for wage earners."

"With the help of a good real estate education and professional advisors you can create steady monthly income, reduce your risk, pay less in taxes, make more money with your banker's money and best of all the government helps you," Mr. Roberts concluded.

Rev. Simmons yelled out, "We're here. Prepare for landing." The helicopter banked right and started to descend very smoothly. Below them Ed and Sasha could see a huge estate house with tennis courts and vast stretch of golf courses with golf carts rolling along in the distance. A light thud announced they were back on land.

As the group stepped off of the helicopter pad on the side of the country club a steady stream of people could be seen coming out of the club house toward them.

"John. What is all this?" Rev. Simmons looked like he was about to tear up as old friends came up to him with hugs and congratulations while others were singing "For He's a Jolly Good Fellow".

Mr. Roberts stood in between Ed and Sasha and squeezed them once again and said "Maybe one day we can grow up to be like him".

The group eventually moved back inside the country club with an ever growing crowd of well wishers surrounding the Reverend. Inside the Lee-Lee Simmons' Great Hall was a grand banquet complete with servers in black pants and vest over crisp shirts and red ties.

After everyone ate, the Reverend and Mr. Roberts caught up with Ed and Sasha as they wandered through the mammoth estate house.

Mr. Roberts smiled as he swirled the ice in his drink. "Now it is time for me to go do some investment work with the bulls over there", he said pointing over to the well heeled gentlemen playing cards at a table not to far from the bar.

"Take it easy on them John", Rev. Simmons admonished.

"Of course I will. I have to keep them coming back", Mr. Roberts said with a wink. Turning to Ed and Sasha he said, "You guys make sure you pay attention to the Reverend here so he can tell you the right philosophy for investing. I will be busy taking these guys money whether they want me to or not."

With that Mr. Roberts wheeled around and walked toward the table with a loud sinister laugh.

Chapter 6

The House Always Wins

"He is one in a million", Rev. Simmons sighed. "The question is a million what."

"Thanks for taking time for us. Especially on your special day", said Sasha.

"Yeah. Thanks a billion", agreed Ed with a smile. "But what did Mr. Roberts mean by he will take their money whether they want him to or not? That seems like the best type of investment lesson right there."

"Well let's take a walk and I will explain", said the Reverend gesturing toward the large garden area that lead out to the golf course. "First of all that is high stakes gentlemen's poker and for everyone else at that table it is gambling. For Mr. Roberts it is an investment. Remember the house always wins and he owns the house."

"Oh. I guess he gets money from their membership and the cards keep them coming back", said Sasha.

"That's the way it goes when gambling and many people confuse gambling with investing", said Rev. Simmons. "That is why so many investors are confused because it is such a broad subject. There are dozens of investment products, procedures and types of investors so no one can profess to know it all. So many people just give up or give their money to someone else to invest.

"True investing is a personal plan and not just a product or a hot stock tip. People often focus on the product, like stocks, and the procedure, like trading, but they really don't have a plan.

"Many families are counting on there investments to support them in the future. The problem is that very few of them are well educated in investing. What happens if the market crashes? The government insures your savings but not your investments.

"An educated investor makes money whether the market is going up or crashing down. This investor has the education and experience to understand the business he is investing in and not just go off of a hot stock tip. After all that is what you are investing in...a business. If you do not understand that business then you will have no idea why that stock went up or down. That is true gambling.

The trio walked over to the front edge of the garden that overlooked the golf course. They sat down on a large marble bench facing the garden with the outside rear of the estate house as a backdrop.

"My wife Lee-Lee found this track of land years ago", Rev. Simmons said reminiscing. "She had a vision and pulled it together. We had John come in with his team of developers to work it through. After she passed, I let John buy it from me so he could continue on with the vision. They have done an outstanding job."

"That is easy to see", replied Sasha while taking in the beautiful scenery.

Rev. Simmons continued saying, "Remember that investing in stocks is just one form of investing. A true investor does not get trapped into just one investment vehicle. They stay focused on their personal plan. So real estate, mutual funds or the stock market are just ways to generate wealth but you should not stay so focused on one that you ignore other opportunities.

"You must develop your personal plan first and then determine the type of investment vehicle that is best for you. For example, investing in a business through the stock market requires a lot of reading, studying and professional advice. Real estate investing requires reading, studying and working with a wide variety of professionals. Entrepreneurship requires all of the above plus lots of patience and perseverance.

"Which vehicle you choose depends on the amount of time and resources you have along with your tolerance for each type. The sad thing is that nine out of ten investors do not make money. They make money one day and then give it back a week later. These gamblers do not lose money; they just fail to make money.

"To a true investor investing is an often dull, boring and almost mechanical process of getting rich with a plan that almost guarantees that you will gain wealth. This plan has strategies and formulas. The more financial skills you have the more strategies and formulas you can use to guarantee a return.

"Never look to investing to get rich quick. I often hear people talk about picking stocks like they would talk about picking a race horse. Now guess who always wins?"

"The house", Ed said nodding his head.

"Of course", said the Reverend. "In this case it could be the brokerage house that calls with a high pressure sells pitch about the latest hot stock tip or the online trading house that places your bets. Even if the stock tanks the brokerage house wins."

A look of concern came over Sasha's face. "So how do you know who to trust?"

"Like everything else in your financial life you need to have a team to work with. This includes a financial planner, banker, accountant, lawyer, broker, bookkeeper, insurance agent and successful mentor. The team approach helps you sort through different issues from various angles to come to the right decisions. But even still, if you want to be rich it does not matter if you work for someone else or for yourself; you've got to mind your own financial business.

"So you need to invest your time into your investments and get professionals to input there time also", Sasha added.

"Well said Sasha. I knew there was a reason why I like you", the Reverend said while giving her a one armed squeeze. "Time is always more valuable than money. If I gave you a billion dollars right before you died, then it would be completely useless to you. So the real investment in wealth is your time educating yourself.

"Many people want to be rich but they are not willing to invest the time. They buy into the get rich quick schemes or start their business without the basic skills. They are in so much of a hurry that they soon lose both time and money.

"The secret of investing is to take the time to develop a long term plan that you can follow. Anyone in the western world can become a millionaire by just doing that. We always hear about the guys who seemingly did it overnight because it makes for sensational news. However the majority of millionaires educated themselves on how to work there plan and took the time to make there plans work.

Sasha asked, "So you had a plan to become a billionaire when you started?"

"My plan wasn't to become a billionaire. I wanted to be financially free. But along the way I learned that you have to continually update your financial knowledge base. After awhile I just became good at creating wealth and keeping it. It is not that I am a genius or anything but if you study long enough you just become good at whatever you do. Bakers bake...I generate wealth.

"As you can see with me and Mr. Roberts, there are different ways and styles of creating wealth. He walks in the room with his flamboyance and people just throw deals at him simply because he looks like he can finance them. I walk in the room and no one really notices. We have different paths but always the same goal...financial freedom.

"Tell us more about creating a personal plan", Ed requested.

"It does take time to create a detailed personal financial plan. It also should include professionals to guide you in your particular circumstances. But it generally requires a plan that first makes you financially secure which means something that is sure to bring you an income and is not too risky.

"The next step is to have a plan that makes you comfortable. This plan is more focused around your savings and to make sure that when you go to the next step of the plan you are not taking high or emotional risk because you feel pressured.

"The last step in the plan is to become financially wealthy. It is important that you have those first two plans in place and working. Plus the plan to become wealthy requires the most study. To get to this level takes many years because the kinds of investments you will be making are going to require a high degree of sophistication and a tolerance for the large financial losses which are going to come. But if you are secure and comfortable those losses will just be learning mistakes and not financial disasters.

"Most wealthy people start there children's financial and investment education early by setting up an investment portfolio. Then they guide them in learning to become investors. That is what I did for my children and that is what they are doing for the grandkids.

"That is the way it will have to be with all children or they won't be able to last in this economy. The creditors and lenders have had hundreds of years to figure out how to get to your money. You only have one lifetime and the earlier you figure it out the better.

"The thing I want you kids to remember is that investing is not risky...it is the investor who is risky if they have not made themselves financially literate or just trust their money to others without finding out what is really going on. Being financially literate is one of the most important investor basics, especially if you want to be a safe investor, an inside investor, and a wealthy investor. Being an investor is not risky. Not being financially literate is."

"Besides Ed, you have the best investment of all", the Reverend continued. "Well aside from Sasha you have your own business. That is how roughly 80% of the very rich became rich. You are concentrating on developing an asset and not just on getting money. With that knowledge not only can you create other businesses but you can also evaluate another business with an insider's eye that most investors do not have."

Ed grinned from ear to ear. "I'm glad I am getting something out of this other than just random headaches."

The three of them sat quietly as a breeze swept through the garden making all of the exotic plants and shrubs sway gently.

"Well tomorrow you two will get a look at how you can continue your financial education", the Reverend said as he leaned back with his eyes closed. "Don't forget to bring your note pads because it is going to be a doosey."

Chapter 7

The Financial Soul Institute

On Thursday, Ed and Sasha had an uneventful exit off of the elevator but what lay in front them was a completely different 20th floor. The same relaxed home office look of Rev. Simmons' 35th floor was there with a few more semi-private areas surrounded by small tables and chairs.

To the left were two large open styled conference areas with seats arranged neatly around tables. There was enough space in between the sections to have a comfortable meeting of 20 to 30 people with out creating a disturbance. In one section most of the chairs were filled and more were being added to accommodate the crowd of people calmly gathered around.

As they looked at the group of people, Ed and Sasha saw Rev. Simmons waving at them and gesturing for them to come over. As they made their way toward him, Bobby came running at them out of nowhere and grabbed Ed's hand.

"Good morning Mr. Ed and Ms. Sasha. Come sit with us", Bobby said as he started dragging Ed like a rag doll toward the Reverend. Sasha saw Doris, Michelle and Cathy sitting down near the table as she tried to keep up with Ed and Bobby.

Sasha smiled as she exchanged hugs with the ladies. "It is so good to see you. What are you guys doing up here?"

"Oh girl, we have so much to talk about", Michelle whispered urgently as a gentleman announced the beginning of the meeting. "Hopefully we will see you after this wraps up".

"Ok", Sasha whispered back. "I'll come back over here".

With that Sasha stepped quickly over to join Bobby, Rev. Simmons and Ed seated near the front row of the table.

The Reverend leaned over and patted Sasha on the hand as she sat down. He looked over the group, then looked back at Ed and Sasha and winked saying, "I set this up just for you two".

Sarah walked in from the side and confidently stepped up in front of the 32 odd people seated in front of her to a loud applause. She wore a sharp yet conservative blue suit pants outfit that was complimented by nicely appointed accessories.

Behind her was a large purple banner that had stitched in it a large circular golden crest with Financial Soul Institute worded on the outside. Inside the crest was a penny on the top left, a simple drawing of a house on the top right and on the bottom was a simple abstract drawing of a cradled baby.

"Good morning family", she said speaking very clearly. "I want to welcome our Financial Soul Members and our honored guest to a special session. We normally have classes on Saturdays at 11:00 AM sharp but we are happy to give life changing financial information to folks whenever we can and it certainly is a pleasure to have all of you here.

"My name is Sarah Bouleware and for a great many years of my life I have lived with a financial mis-education that kept me locked in a cycle of work and debt that sucked up my time and left me with just stuff and bills.

"With the correct money education and support of the Financial Soul Institute I was able to move completely out of debt, start my own business and put myself in a position were my family is literally financially free. Today I want to share some information with you that could put you in that position or make you even more financially secure. Is that OK?"

The group nodded in agreement.

Sarah continued saying, "We have a very important topic to cover today so let's get started. Everyone please hold up your program".

Sasha held hers up with the crowd as Ed looked around for his and then realized he was sitting on it.

"In this program is valuable information about what we are going to cover today which is debt management but also information on upcoming classes, books we recommend for your financial growth and conference calls that will be held during the week and their topics.

"Just as important are the businesses and services located toward the back of the program. Normally we have anyone who would like to stand and introduce themselves and their business, service or potential business or service so that we all can network together. Since we have such a large crowd, I will mention the businesses in the program and ask that the business owner or business team stand so that you can be recognized. Please hold your applause to the end".

Without the aid of notes, Sarah named 5 businesses with a brief description. One of the businesses Sarah announced was, "DMC Healthy Brown Bag Lunches, Inc. – Healthy Taste That Fit Your Time - headed by the team of Doris Knowles, Michelle Combs, and Cathy Carter". Ed and Sasha couldn't wait to start clapping after the last company was named.

After the applause, Sarah continued, "We want your mind, heart and spirit to be open to what you are about to hear so we always start our meetings with the Statement of Financial Commitment. Everyone please join us by standing, pointing your right finger to your head and repeat after me.

My Financial Commitment
I commit to studying wealth
Learning wealth
Gaining wealth
Using wealth and
Sharing wealth

"Thank you and please be seated. Today we are going to cover a topic that I am sure affects just about everyone in this room and definitely someone that you know. It is debt. Now I have a question, who do you work for?"

After a moment of murmuring quiet an anonymous voice said "John". Ripples of light laughter swept through the audience.

Sarah answered, "I know Mr. Roberts pretty well and I am quite sure he would not agree with you. In fact, he would say you first work for yourself; otherwise you would not take a paycheck. Then he would say you work for whoever you owe money to. Your mortgage company, school loans, credit cards, car loans or any other debt you owe. After that you work for your family.

"It may be hard to accept but look at how you live if you owe money. YOU get the paycheck for your work to pay all of your DEBTORS and then you squeeze in time for your FAMILY before you go back to work for your DEBTORS.

"Another way to look at it is to see retirement as being able to spend as much time with your family as possible, Sarah continued. "Can you retire with debt?"

There was an anxious silence in the crowd.

"The answer is no. Just as it was when you were working you can not spend more than your income without going into further debt. And obviously, you are not going to gain more income while retired than when you worked. So kiss your remaining family time good bye as you get ready to look for a new job or continue working at the old one to pay back your debts."

Sarah walked slowly around the tables as she spoke. "Look, there are not too many things I am going to say about your financial future that you have not stayed up at night more than a few times thinking about. But let's look at the most common debt relief programs that can get you into more debt and then go into the proper process to get you out of debt. Is that alright?"

Audience members nodded with several folks saying "Yes please".

Sarah turned, walked back towards the front and said, "Now this is something that is important to remember. If you have an income and you have a debt problem, then income is not your problem…cash flow management is your problem.

"Often when people go into debt, the first thing they do is look for another job. Well that is great except the exact same problems you had before will come back again. You have not addressed the real problems of your financial situation with education so you can actually get more money and end up in more debt.

"Being financially undereducated is risky and unfortunately this has been going on for years. Prior to the baby boom starting in 1946 debtors were seen as unworthy or unfit because they were obviously not able to provide for themselves or their family meaning they had to borrow money just to get by.

"Now carrying anchors of debt is not only normal…it is highly encouraged. The encouragement is coming from the creditors and the financial industry as a whole. Since most people do not have their own financial plan, they laid one out for them. The plan is for you to retire broke or work until the day you die and they become multi-millionaires on your money.

As Sarah walked around the group she stopped and put her hands on the shoulders of an older gentleman wearing a nice suit and a very loud tie. "I want to introduce you guys to Sal Emerson. He is our resident mortgage expert and he is going to break down some of the issues surrounding one of your biggest expenses. Sal the floor is yours."

"Hey folks", Sal said as he stood and walked towards the front. "I have been in the industry for a long time and there are two things you need to understand. One is that there are a lot of great people who really care about their customers. The other thing is that it is a part of their job to get as much money from you as they legally and ethically can.

"I mean that is the way it is with any service or product. If a guy charges you $30 more to fix your plumbing because you don't know any better, he isn't really being mean…he just wants to put food on the table for his kids.

"The point is that you need to know what is going on with your money. Especially with purchases like $300,000 that can affect your debt for years to come. So I appreciate the opportunity to talk to you guys.

"Let's look at what could be the biggest drain on your finances. If you had a $150,000 mortgage that you just refinanced at 6%, it would mean your 30 year mortgage payment is $899.33. Which really means your house is really going to cost you $323,758.80. Even after tax break of $57,000 the house still cost you $266,418.

"So you are paying $116,418 more for your house. Does that make sense to you? It does to your lenders. To make matters worse the finance industry invests your $899.33 mortgage payment to earn a return by handing you credit cards. If you have a mortgage payment and a credit card, then someone's hand is very deep into your pockets.

"But wait. Don't think you are going to get off that easy. The Mortgage Industry has made it very difficult for people to resist the temptation of pulling every bit of equity available out of a piece of property. The refinancing of existing mortgages has become the norm. Now paying off your mortgage and owning your own home before death or retirement has become a thing of the past.

"Not every mortgage is designed for you. We recommend a fixed rate were the term interest rate and amortized monthly payment is predictable. A variable rate mortgage means your monthly payment can fluctuate. An interest only mortgage is contractually a temporary loan and best suited for real estate investors because it was never designed for the average consumer.

"There are hundreds of other mortgage packages out there that were created by professional lenders to generate as much of a profit for themselves as they legally can. It is your responsibility to be just as educated as they are. After all it will be you who will have to live with paying that note.

"I will be sticking around after we are finished here if you have any questions. Remember when you are talking about a mortgage is important to have someone on your side to help."

"Thanks Sal", Sarah said as the audience clapped and Sal took his seat.

"When it comes to getting out of debt, the only true solution is financial knowledge", said Sarah. "Everyday that you live according to how your creditors have planned is another day you will end up owing them more. Your creditors want your ignorance to work for them. Let's get your money intelligence to work for you."

"I am glad to see so many of you taking notes. So why don't you jot down 'Building Your Debt Plan'."

"Your debt plan starts by looking at your creditor's plan", continued Sarah. Using your credit card, mortgage, car loan or any other debt statements you can pull out your principle balance, interest rate, and monthly payment. With that information you can add up all of your current payments to determine your monthly debt budget.

"You can now also calculate your debt free date and the total amount of interest you will be giving to your creditors. With this information in your hands you can create your own debt plan. Now lets talk about which debt elimination plan will make the most sense for you.

Sarah asked the crowd, "Are you guys still with me?"

A resounding "Yes" came back from the crowd.

"Great! Remember even if this does not apply to you right now, you may have children, family or friends who may need this information. Ok, you can go ahead and jot down...'Just Spend More Money'."

"This is the plan that most people automatically fall back on. Just pay more and you will be out of debt faster. While yes this strategy definitely works, unfortunately, most people who are in debt don't have the extra funds to keep up with this plan so it becomes unpredictable and inefficient. Has anyone tried this approach for a couple of months and then got off track?"

Scattered yeses could be heard throughout the group and quite a few hands went up.

"Well I have too", said Sarah. "So let's keep looking for a plan that works by checking out the 'Debt Consolidation Loan'.

"Please pay attention to this because this is the most popular and most damaging plan. You guys have seen the commercials. This is actually a debt enlargement plan because they give you a new loan with lower monthly payments. However this just stretches out your payments and adds thousands to hundreds of thousands more in interest. All they are doing is selling you a new loan. Do not get caught in this trap.

"While there are even more new programs coming out to try to save you by putting you into more debt, just remember this...any debt reduction plan that involves a new loan is not a program designed to get you out of debt. Ok let's move on to the next area which is the 'Credit Counseling Program'."

"People are often confused by the Credit Counseling Programs out there so here is the long and short of it. Credit counseling is required before filing for bankruptcy. This is mandated by the Federal Government. These plans are an alternative to filing for bankruptcy but this plan has it problems too.

"Although these are non-profit agencies, there have been cases of fraud. The consumer basically grants the agency control of a portion of their income to make sure their creditors are paid on time. The agency attempts to work with the creditors to get better terms and interest rates but there are no guarantee that this will happen."

The screens changed once again with 'Snowball Planning' popping up. Sarah continued talking.

"The Snowball Plan is a great plan for saving time and interest but it does have some drawbacks that you should be aware of. The basics of this plan are to reduce all of your monthly expenditures to a minimum, line up your debts by their balance from the lowest to the highest. Then you simply go after your smallest balance first to pay it off and then go after your next lowest balance. You continue with this plan until you pay off all of your debts.

"Of course with anything dealing with creditors you want to use a high degree of financial knowledge to keep the most money you can so nothing is ever quite so simple. This strategy does not take into account the fact that every debt is different depending on the principle balance, interest rate and monthly balance. Any changes in these three areas can alter the best strategy for saving the most money. Using the snowball affect by itself is almost never the fastest and most effective way out of debt.

"Stay with me now and write down 'Financial Knowledge at Work'."

"We feel the best strategy for getting out of debt is to take the best of these plans and remove the worst parts. This new strategic plan covers all aspects of your debt including your creditors plan, your debt plan and creating a plan that can tell you the exact date you will be out of debt and even the exact debt you can become a millionaire. This comprehensive plan is easy to follow and flexible to allow for the inevitable changes in life.

"First you start by analyzing the creditors plan which will let you know the exact Day, Month and Year that each of your current debts will be paid off with the current balance, interest rate and monthly payment.

"Next, while working within that budget you can put together a debt elimination plan using a similar philosophy to Snowballing. But this time using the principle balance, interest rate and payment structure the correct order of payment can be established to accelerate the elimination of all of the debts as quickly as possible.

"After that you will be able to see how much power your income has each and every month. Once you are debt free, based on an assumed rate of return, you can calculate the Day, Month and Year you will become a cash millionaire just by paying yourself instead of you creditors.

"If you would like help, we have teamed up with professional advisors who can reduce the number of complex calculations and guide you in creating your plan. They can also e-mail you every month a simple 2 page summary showing all key aspects with easy to follow instructions. Plus they give you an updated debt elimination date. Now you have a goal you can see for getting out of debt which helps you stick to your plan.

"Of course this plan has the flexibility to deal with any additional debts, refinances or emergencies and can be updated to keep you in the know on track to your debt free and millionaire dates."

Sarah stood in front of the table with the same enthusiasm that she started with and asked, "Did you learn something new that could add to your money education?"

The audience responded with a loud a loud applause punctuated with shouts "Yes" and "Thank you Sarah" added in from people who were writing furiously on note pads.

"If you learned something, anything at all, about the mortgage industry and debt solutions then please tell your friends and family and to invite them to any of our free financial education seminars. For us, this is a crusade to stop people from losing time with their loved ones simply because they do not have the correct information", Sarah continued. "Is that alright with you guys?"

Once again there was a loud applause.

"Obviously I can not possibly cover all of the information that you would need to make personal changes to your financial life in this little bit of time. That is why we stress continual financial education in groups of supportive people.

"For the next half an hour, we are going to break up into groups so you can find out more information for the particular financial issue you want to tackle". Sarah gestured to the three people in the group that raised their hands, "Just talk to one of our Financial Soul Stewards in the debt, real estate and entrepreneur sections and they will take care of you.

"I want to thank all of you for coming out today. I look forward to seeing you tomorrow, with a friend of course, for another presentation with a very special guest speaker who will talk to us about the Power of Appreciation. You will not want to miss this.

"Thanks again and have a rewarding day", Sarah concluded.

As the crowd applauded and drifted off into their sections, Ed and Sasha joined the swarm of well wishers who surrounded Sarah and congratulated her on a job well done. Bobby held Sarah's hand and seemed to enjoy the appreciation as much as his mother.

Ed and Sasha caught up to Michelle, Doris and Cathy over by the entrepreneurs section as they filled out a survey asking for the type of financial information they needed for their business.

Sasha gave each one of them a congratulatory hug and teased, "Can I place an order for a brown bag lunch?"

"You most certainly can", Michelle said happily. "We got three orders from the people sitting around us. That was great marketing for us and it was free."

"Oh the timing for all of this is just perfect", exclaimed Doris. "I don't know if we would have been able to deal with everything that has happened in the past three days."

"After our conversation on Monday, we were just so depressed we decided that we had to do something. So we met up that night and decided to work together with Michele's idea", Cathy added.

"That is wonderful", said Ed. "Marketing is one of the biggest factors in the success of a business and the costliest. You guys are off to a good start. I wonder what made the Financial Soul people do all of this?"

"You guys didn't hear?" Doris leaned in to Ed and Sasha and said quietly, "John is selling the business to a group of investors. Everyone is terrified about what is going to happen next. The memo that went out yesterday said that the new owners have not said they were going to do any lay offs but you know how that goes. Mr. Roberts highly suggested that I come to this meeting today with some co-workers. He let me know this was going to happen Tuesday so I got our name into the program early."

"I am sorry to hear that he is selling the company", said Sasha. "Hopefully everything will work out."

"Hope is great but the mortgage payment is expected", replied Cathy. "I may not have cared too much for Mr. Roberts but at least I knew that I had a job with great benefits. He kept this company going even through all these changes. Now I just don't know."

Ed and Sasha nodded quietly.

"I relate so much with everything that Sarah said", Michelle sighed. "I feel like I am being set up to be used by spending thousands of dollars even though I don't have to. Its like if you don't know the ins and outs of money then at some point someone is going rip it right out of your hand. I am in the middle of trying to buy a house and I feel so alone. They have accountants, lawyers and lenders on their side. I have never bought a house before. How am I supposed to know what is going on with that mountain of paperwork they keep throwing at me?"

With that Michelle handed her survey to Doris and said, "That reminds me. I have to go over to the real estate side. Please turn this in for me."

Michelle wheeled around and bumped right into Rev. Simmons.

"I am glad to see you are excited about protecting your money Michelle", the Reverend said with a smile. "But take your time. We want you to be in one piece."

Michelle apologized and left to make her way through the crowd.

Ed asked, "Do you know everyone in the building?"

"You get to know a lot of people when you're a janitor", replied the Reverend. "Isn't that right ladies?"

"That's right Rev. Simmons", replied Doris and Cathy together as they gave him a hug.

"Do you mind if I borrow these two youngsters from you? They have some more things to learn before we let them go this week", said Rev. Simmons.

Ed and Sasha wished the ladies good luck and walked back to the office with the billionaire janitor.

Chapter 8

The State of the Financials

In the office, Ed and Sasha were greeted by Sarah and Bobby who sat at the counter with a coloring book. Sarah walked over to the sofa, took her shoes off and collapsed on it.

"I love doing this but it takes so much out of me", Sarah said.

"Well you did a great job. There is so much that I must learn and you really inspired me to find out more", said Sasha.

"Hey don't forget you old mentors." Ed and Sasha looked up to see Mr. Roberts staring at the children's drawings on the walls. He was still dressed to the nines but for the first time he did not have his tie all the way up, the top buttons were open and his shirt sleeves were rolled up.

"I don't think anyone can forget the two greatest money mentors in the world", replied Sarah.

Sasha sat down next to Sarah and asked, "These guys were your mentors too?"

"Oh I would not have learned how to get out from under my financial boulder without these two. Actually I don't think I would have realized that there was a boulder at all", said Sarah.

While pulling glasses from the cabinet, Rev. Simmons added, "Most people don't realize that they are even in financial hot water until it is too late. It's like putting a frog in cold water and then turning on the heat. The frog will slowly start boiling and not even know it. Of course, if you tried to throw the frog in boiling water it would automatically try to jump out."

"I guess I got thrown in the boiling pot at a young age so it is hard for me to understand how people can't see why they are constantly losing everything they have worked for", said Mr. Roberts without removing his eyes from the artwork.

"That is why you have us around", replied the Reverend as he handed Mr. Roberts a glass. "There is nothing but sweet tea in there by the way."

"I knew there was something that looked different about you", teased Sasha. "No martini glass? It is going on 12:00."

"Hey, have some sympathy. I just sold my business and lost 5,000 of my adopted children. I may have been the mean step dad but my kids always had a meal at the table. But I could not have kept it up. The world is changing and I am getting a little too tired to change with it", said Mr. Roberts looking down and sighing.

"Oh, I really didn't mean to offend you Mr. Roberts", Sasha offered. "I mean it was…"

"Ha ha! Fooled ya", Mr. Roberts yelled as he pulled a flask out of his pocket and poured some whiskey in his glass. "I just sold the ranch and the cattle have to fend for themselves", he hooted while dancing a jig around in a circle.

"Your not fooling anybody you big softy", Sarah yelled back from the sofa laughing. "You know you are going to miss taking care of your little ones and your precious company. You are just going to worry about them from a distance now."

"Yeah, yeah…whatever", grumbled Mr. Roberts with a smile while taking a sip from his glass. "That is someone else's problem now."

Ed grinned and asked, "Is that why you set up the class this morning?"

"That is what he needs us for. To teach all of those employees how to fend for themselves", Sarah said.

Sasha perked up on the sofa and asked, "But what is it that they don't know that has kept them in…I can't believe I am going to say this…cattle mode all these years?"

"Well let's review the secrets before we give you that answer", answered the Reverend.
"What is the secret of money?"

"Compound interest", replied Ed.

"Great", Rev. Simmons enthused. "What is the secret of business?"

"Care about people," Sasha answered quickly.

Mr. Roberts sat down across from Sasha and Sarah taking up the most of the love seat. "And what is the secret of real estate?"

"Leverage", said Sarah.

Rev. Simmons shot back with, "How about the secret to investing?"

"Take the time to develop a long term plan that you can follow", answered Sasha.

"Well done. I see we have all of our prize pupils in the same place today", Rev. Simmons encouraged. "We have been leading you to the answer to this secret all week. Wealth can only be obtained through financial literacy. So what is the secret of personal financial success?"

"Reading financial statements", said Bobby without even looking up from his coloring book.

Everyone turned and stared at Bobby. Sarah jumped up and squealed, "That's my baby! That's my baby!" Mr. Roberts and Rev. Simmons whistled and clapped.

"Like I said, our prize pupils are all in the same place", said Rev. Simmons beaming.

"He is absolutely correct and ahead of nearly 95% of the American population. Even with doctors, lawyers and Indian Chiefs included", said Mr. Roberts. "In school you got a report card that gave you a chance to at least find out how you are doing so that you could make corrections. Out in the real world, the report card for every adult is their financial statement. But most do not even know they need one and the rest would not know how to read one if it was put in front of them."

"Learning how to pull together my personal financial statement and then knowing how to read it saved my financial hide", added Sarah. "Once I could see how I was throwing away my time and money for silly stuff it kept me out of the stores and made me change my priorities. It made me see in plain numbers how I was turning my cash into trash. Now I feel secure knowing that my cash is being turned into assets that can generate even more cash."

"You mean all this time I thought I was financially savvy but I really didn't get it all", said Sasha. "I have never put together or read my own financial statements. The financial statements in the annual reports from the companies I invest in…well…", Sasha looked around sheepishly, "I really just looked to see the executive's salaries.

This got Mr. Roberts rolling with laughter. Wiping tears from his eyes he said, "Oh, I really didn't mean to offend you. Oh that was great. Hee hee hee." Pulling himself back together Mr. Roberts continued, "Look wealth is not a comparison game. Besides, you can't be jealous or spiteful of a person while you are trying to be like them. Your brain doesn't want you to be like someone you hate and will keeping shutting you down from financial success. Plus by the time you make it to their level you will be so pissed off you wouldn't be happy anyway."

"Whether you make $10 an hour or $1000 an hour does not make you make you wealthy if you are not doing what you love or you spend your time worrying about what someone else has got."

"This is true", the Reverend added. "It does not matter how much you make if your financial statement is out of whack. That is what separates the wealthy from everyone else. Understanding a financial statement is how you can identify a risky investment or a sound one."

Mr. Roberts took a sip from his glass and asked, "Do you know who gets a constantly updated financial statement on you that are read by professionals?"

Ed and Sasha just shrugged. The room fell silent as Mr. Roberts eyed the two of them and took another sip.

A small voice could be heard off-handedly saying, "The credit bureau".

Everyone looked up and stared at Bobby again as he busily colored without breaking his concentration.

"I don't know which is scarier", said Sasha. "The answer or that a five year old knows more about this than I do."

"When you guys first came in and said you were worried about your financial future and didn't understand why your business was not growing, we knew right away that you were not aware of your personal financial statements. Understanding a financial statement is the difference between a small business and an established business. Isn't that right Ed?"

"I think this may be the single most important thing I have heard concerning my business", Ed said while contemplating. "I have worked with accountants who have prepared financial statements for me. I could see the numbers and I knew what they meant but I could never read or fully understand the statement. I can see how missing that one element has held me back for so long. Aw man. I just feel like crying."

"Hey look guys. Don't get down on yourselves", said Sarah as she wrapped her arm around Sasha. "You can't get upset about something you were never told you needed to learn. You can't really even blame your teachers or parents. When we say 95% of the population can't read a financial statement that includes them too. Even they were told to just get more money and that will solve the problem."

"Before you can become successful at real estate, investing or business you have to be able to read your own financial statement and then be able to read others. That is how you can tell if you are secure and comfortable to move on to larger investments", added Rev. Simmons.

"Think of investing like buying a car", said Mr. Roberts. "The guy who doesn't know any better will judge the value of a car by the price and how many miles are on it...just like the price of a stock and its price to earnings ratio. A sophisticated investor can use the financial statement to look inside the investment and make a more sound decision...just like an experienced car mechanic will thoroughly go through the car to get the real value and then make a buying decision. Without the financial statement, anything else is just really bad guessing."

"That's a good one Mr. Roberts", exclaimed Sarah. "I am going to have to borrow that from you."

"Feel free, feel free. I also do weddings and bar mitzvahs", Mr. Roberts joked. "But seriously my first lesson in the importance of a personal financial statement came from my old boss who my father had worked for. When I went to him to ask for funds to help me purchase stock in this company, he looked over the companies financial statements and then asked for my personal financial statement. I replied that I didn't have one.

"He told me that I must not be able to read the company financial statement myself and that all I was asking him to do was to gamble on a bad gambler. Two months later after an intense education on creating my own financial statements and reading a company statement he gave me the money." Mr. Roberts spread his arms wide and said, "That was my largest investment and the rest is a multi-millionaire's history."

"Wow that is some story", Ed marveled.

"The point is that without that education in financial statements I am quite sure I would have blown his investment and everyone else who invested with me", Mr. Roberts replied. "Isn't that right Rev?"

"That is the story for me and Lee-Lee too. We studied with John and invested with him. That one introduction to financial statements literally built everything around you right now", said Rev. Simmons.

Bobby hopped down off the stool and presented his drawing to Rev. Simmons. "Can this picture go on the wall too?"

The Reverend showed the picture to group. It was the Financial Soul logo with the penny, house and baby.

Everyone clapped and added "We have an artist in the house", "Way to go Bobby", "Let me get a copy".

Bobby gave a little bow and ran over with Rev. Simmons to get a frame for the wall.

Ed asked Sarah, "What does that logo mean?"

"Well it symbolizes what is really important in your financial world. Security is in the penny. If you can appreciate a penny then you are ready for your millions. Comfort is in the house. Your best decisions can be made when you are comfortable and have the time to plan and think things through. The baby symbolizes wealth. Babies just naturally enjoy their time with the person around them which is true wealth."

"Oh yeah. That's good 'n deep", replied Ed.

"Sometimes it seems that finance is so complicated and at other times it seems so easy", wondered Sasha.

"You deal with money everyday. If you understand what you is dealing with then you practice correctly everyday. It does not take too long to get it right once you get the basics down. Everything else is apple tarts and cream…or whiskey depending on how you look at it", said Mr. Roberts with a wink.

"Well in the meantime, we need to prepare for tomorrow", Sarah said as she stood up. "You guys better get some rest. I am sure there will be quite a few surprises."

"There always is around this place", replied Ed as he and Sasha prepared to leave.

Chapter 9

The Power of Appreciation

On Friday, Ed and Sasha rode up on a packed elevator to the 35th floor. They stepped off the elevator and paused to take in the floor that just seemed to be engulfed with people. To the left there was ampitheater style seating with a riser and a podium. On the right, all of the desk and couches had been removed and another seating area was set up facing 3 large screen TVs. There was no riser in this overflow area.

Sasha spotted Michelle and waved to her asking, "What is going on? Who are all of these people?"

"Mr. Roberts has given each section of the company time off from work with pay to come to these seminars", replied Michelle. "It looks like everyone is taking advantage. I know I need it.

Suddenly Ed felt a quick tug on his pants. He looked down to see Bobby. "Good Morning, Mr. Ed and Ms. Sasha. Come sit with us."

Ed looked at Sasha and whispered, "This kid needs to stop hanging with Mr. Roberts and the Reverend. Now they have him sneaking up on us."

Sasha laughed, said goodbye to Michelle and grabbed Bobby's hand as he weaved their way through the crowd. Bobby pulled them to three empty seats near the front of the overflow area.

As they began to sit down a tall handsome gentleman stood up and introduced himself. "Hello, I'm Ken Bouleware, Bobby's dad. You must be Ed and Sasha. I have heard so much about you guys from Bobby and Sarah.

Sasha smiled and said, "It is really a pleasure to meet you. You guys have a very smart young man here. Let me know when he is ready to do taxes."

Music could be heard in the background as everyone in the crowd headed to their seats and got ready for the presentation to begin. The lights began to dim and the TV screens came on with the Financial Soul logo floating across. From the across the room near the stage you could hear an applause building. Suddenly, on all five monitors, you could see Sarah walking onto the stage.

Bobby pointed excitedly and said, "Look Daddy. It's Mommy on TV."

Ken answered, "I see Bobby. Doesn't mommy look pretty?"

As the warm applause died down, Sarah began by saying, "Welcome back to day two of our special presentation. I am glad so many of you brought your friends with you. Not only because it is important for everyone to have as much financial knowledge as possible but also because we have an outstanding speaker today who bring decades of experience and education in gaining and keeping wealth."

"I don't want to keep you from one moment of time with him so let's get started. First please hold your programs up."

This time Ed was ready with his.

"Please read through this for very valuable information on financial topics and resources you can use today. We also have businesses and services listed on the back. If you are going to spend money it might as well be within a community that supports you. Isn't that right?"

The audience agreed with nods of the heads and "That's right".

Sarah continued saying, "Of course, those who have been here before know the routine. For our new guest, we always start our meetings with the Statement of Financial Commitment. Everyone please join us by standing, pointing your right finger to your head and repeat after me."

My Financial Commitment
I commit to studying wealth
Learning wealth
Gaining wealth
Using wealth
Enjoying wealth and
Sharing wealth"

"Thank you and please be seated. Now I am going to bring up a man who everyone in here probably knows in some shape or fashion since his great reputation does precede him. He is the leader of the Financial Soul Institute. He not only builds buildings but also builds communities. He prides himself on building wealth and excels at sharing it. He is humble enough to clean up your working house and smart enough to clean up your financial house. Ladies and gentlemen please join me in welcoming your friend and mine Rev. Simmons."

The crowd gave an excited standing ovation with loud shouts of "Good morning Reverend" ringing throughout as Rev. Simmons stepped on the stage. When he appeared on the monitors the applause from the overflow audience grew.

"Thank you. Thank you family", Rev. Simmons said over the crowd. "Thank you very much and thank you too Sarah. With that introduction I thought somebody else was about to come up here."

As the crowd settled back down, Rev. Simmons spoke with a somber voice. "I don't want to waste a second of your time because we have some very troubling problems in our community that need to be addressed right now. Somewhere along the line in this country we have lost sight of what it means to live free and even more troubling is that we have lost sight of each other.

"Most people are stuck in a world of working for money and not for each other. Money is just a symbol of stored energy. You give energy to a job and you are rewarded with money. Of course there is nothing wrong with that until you give your money, meaning your stored time and money, away without understanding where it is going.

"Did you know that in 2006 more Americans went into bankruptcy than got divorced, graduated or got cancer? That means our sickly, uneducated broken homes are now being financially destroyed too.

"Today's family has less money than they did 30 years ago. Many are paying off debt by getting into even more debt. To make matters worse, credit card fees have gone up160% in the last five years. On top of that, credit card companies will try to make you late on payments by delaying the processing of your payments and sending you the notices late.

"And just when you thought the deck was stacked up against you as high as possible these credit card companies go after your child in college and focus on the people in the worst financial positions like bankruptcy because they know that they make the best late paying customers. These companies actually make 33% of their revenues from late fees and the high interest rates that go along with them.

Rev. Simmons stepped down off the riser and walked down the front aisle gently touching the shoulder of each person as he walked by for emphasis as he made a point, "Do not think that you are safe from these practices. When one person goes down financially, we all take the hit.

"Sub-prime mortgages were not designed for the average consumer. A sophisticated real estate investor can use a sub-prime loan when they know they are not going to hold on to a property long enough to ever get to a balloon payment.

"At least the average consumer would be savvy enough to see that this mortgage package could be dangerous. Well someone got the bright idea to give it to the below average consumer who obviously had problems paying on time because they had low credit scores.

"Now why would they do that? Why? Anyone?" The Reverend spotted someone with their hand up and quickly pointed to him. "Ralph, please help us understand.

Ralph stood up and said loudly, "Because they can still make a ton of money off of the backs of people that can barely pay them. Money illiterate people make the best suckers."

A low murmur went through the crowd as they absorbed what was just said.

"They can still make a ton of money off of the backs of these people that can barely pay", repeated the Reverend as he lowered his voice. "But I have to disagree with Ralph slightly and I want everyone to pay attention.

"When these sub-prime mortgages hit foreclosure in your neighborhood the property value goes down for everyone. When a string of foreclosures hit the city, the city tax base goes down. When the state has to scramble to provide services for the folks affected, your state gets a financial hit.

"The overall drag on the economy and the weakening dollar means people from other countries can buy houses in the US and rent them back to our citizens. Ladies and gentlemen no matter how you look at it, YOU just got hit. Money illiteracy has made us a nation of suckers.

"But these situations are actually the symptoms of a much more devilish problem. Under the right circumstances, when a person lends you money it can be a powerful way to increase you ability to investment in real estate, start a business or be used in so many other positive ways.

"So let's get to the 'why' of the situation. Why are so many people in debt? Why did they take the money to begin with? Why would anyone buying something knowing they don't have the money for it? Why could that even possibly make sense to them?

"Let's look at the greatest force your financial soul has and it is called the Power of Appreciation." Rev. Simmons stepped back on the stage and stood behind the podium. For the first time, the Reverend actually looked like a Reverend to Ed and Sasha.

"If there is any one thing that determines where you are right now and your ability to get to where you want to go in life it is appreciation", he continued. "Appreciation is something that is applied in the financial world to make an asset increase in value. When you apply this principle to your financial soul and use it in your everyday life it has the power to make you wealthy instantaneously because you will immediately see wealth all around you.

"Let's break this down to see where the power in it lies. An asset is something that already has some value. Your house, clothes, food, and even your paycheck are assets. Even if you do not own it but it is available to you, then it is still an asset to you. The public library is an easy example of something that has value that you can use freely.

"Many people do not appreciate what is around them right now. So what they have around them are things that are in a constant cycle of depreciation. Depreciation in your life is nasty and vicious because it is a living curse that not only affects you and your possessions but it also affects the people around you.

"The reason why it is a living curse is because you stop rejoicing in what you have and start to blindly grab for something you don't have in a constant attempt at immediate temporary satisfaction.

"People often pray for a big payday someday and are not being thankful for the payment they are receiving right now. Therefore they do not see the value of that asset, ignore it and allow it to depreciate. God won't give you something you can't handle and that includes more money. If you are running away from your current blessing, then how can you appreciate the next one? It will simply go right past you.

"If you can imagine death walking through a forest, then you can see the grass, trees and flowers withering and dying with every step it takes. It is removing life. It is depreciating value.

Is that what we do with our paycheck? Do we get it and immediately kill it? Which makes us run away from it? In order to break the paycheck to paycheck cycle you must appreciate what has already been given to you. Otherwise you will be right back were you started from...just older.

"The bills may be different, the lifestyle, circumstances, people around you, car you drive, etc, etc, etc. But the cycle is still the same. If you are financially crippled today, chances are you were like that last week, last year and for the last decade. And absolutely no one can break that cycle but you.

"If you looked up appreciation is the encyclopedia, it will tell you to also see investing, gratitude and marketing. That is very interesting because when you appreciate anything you are investing your energy in it. Notice that you do not have to always invest money to increase its value...more times than not your energy is enough.

"The way you focus your energy into something is to first be grateful for it. Gratitude is not only an emotion but also a thankful way of thinking and it is reciprocating to a favor that has been done to you. In other words, gratitude it is a verb. When you are thankful then you use your energy to do something about it. Research shows that people who show gratitude more often are also happier, more helpful and forgiving, and less depressed than less grateful people.

"Marketing is a key component of appreciation because it controls your perception. The reason why some kids will continually want to get the latest toy is simply because someone else marketed it to them. They gave the kid the perception that the new toy has more value than the old toy. So the new toy is worth the kid's appreciation and money. The old toy which already has real value because it has been paid for starts to immediately depreciate in the kid's perception.

"Now check this out", Rev. Simmons said lowering his voice and leaning in like he was telling a secret, "You can replace the kid in this example with adults."

As Rev. Simmons paused for dramatic affect, a light "Aaaaahh" came from the crowd as some people realized what he was getting at.

"How many of you have a car that is less than three years old with a car note? Don't raise your hands; I just want you to think about this. If you had a car that worked and then for some strange reason you just had to have that new car, then someone marketed it to you and changed your perception.

Well according to the Power of Appreciation you are now giving your energy to someone else, in the form of working to pay for that car, instead of appreciating what you had and keeping that energy to yourself.

"I want to make sure you understand this because you will have to work an additional three to five years or however long your car note is for something you already had simply because someone else changed your mind. Some people would say that the new car is safer. Let me tell you something, the only safe car is a car that is paid for.

"Check this out", Rev. Simmons said clapping his hands for emphasis, "Everyone knows that a new or used car depreciates in value when it rolls off the lot. But it actually appreciates in value to you as soon as it is paid for. Now if you are grateful for this car and invest energy into it by simply taking care of it, at some point it will actually appreciate in value to others also because it is perceived as a classic.

"Remember that something that is classic has just kept its value long enough that it starts to appreciate. Within the definition of gratitude is the word reciprocate. When you give energy to something and it appreciates then that energy comes back to you and adds value to you.

"If you want to get off the financial treadmill then stop being a consumer and start being an appreciator."

Many in the audience nodded their heads while taking notes.

"If you want to feel the real differences, please say this out loud", Rev. Simmons cleared his voice and continued. "I appreciate myself".

The crowd responded with a loud "I appreciate myself".

Rev. Simmons smiled and then said, "Now say I consume myself".

"I consume myself", came back from the audience along with laughter.

"That doesn't even sound right does it? To make the power of appreciation work for you, you have to market to yourself. Your perception of anything that you bought should be extremely high because it represents your valuable time. It represents the time you took away from your family and friends. It represents the time you took away from being able to take care of yourself so you can work.

"The more you appreciate what you have the more time you have. The more you try to consume what you don't have the less time you have. Spending money needlessly means that you have to work needlessly.

Then the Reverend said, "Now touch your neighbor and say, 'I need my time, so I can't consume myself'".

The audience smiled and grinned as they complied.

Rev. Simmons continued, "So how do we change?"

"The first thing is to become an appreciator and realize that appreciation is a mindset and a lifestyle. It is also a living testimonial. People like to be around appreciators simply because, like I said earlier, they are grateful, happier and nicer to be around.

"Appreciation takes smiling, study, focus, interest and discipline. Smiling is the real secret of appreciating anything. Think of what you want to appreciate, smile and breathe deep. When you smile your brain sends happy signals that add to the feelings about what you want to appreciate. Breathing deep just adds even more fuel to the happy fire. Now you have the emotional energy to invest with your time.

"You have to study whatever you want to appreciate. If you don't you can easily do something stupid that will make what you want to appreciate actually depreciate. Do you have a phone with a whole bunch of functions that you don't know how to use? I saw one of my friends taking pictures with his phone. I decided I wanted that and took my nice phone back to the store to get a new one. The sales lady was trying to sell me a $500 phone when she saw the look of horror on my face and asked "Why do you want to upgrade your phone?" I told her I wanted to take pictures. She simply picked up my old phone took a picture of me and gave it back to me."

"Maybe that shows you how old I am. But it also shows that if you do not study your marriage, money, children, car or anything else you want to appreciate then you can actually do something that will harm your asset. Try giving your wife lingerie that is two sizes to small and see what happens to that asset."

Laughter erupted from the crowd.

Rev. Simmons continued saying, "A great acronym for focus is Follow One Course Until Successful. If you spend money to take a cooking course, then don't quit in the middle to take up the piano. When you appreciate the value that the course will bring to you and your family then keep going until you are a fabulous cook. If it gets tough then smile, breathe deep and stay focused.

"Interest is another financial term that is used in the Power of Appreciation. Interest is the earning of capital, particularly the price paid for the use of an asset over a given period of time. But here is another way to look at it. In medieval times, time was considered to be the property or an asset of God. In other words, interest is the price you pay for using God's time to make your investment grow. Show no interest…see no growth.

"So if you show interest in your child, you are using God's time to help her grow. Anything you want to grow, show interest in and it will appreciate. This is where the actual power in the Power of Appreciation comes from. It applies to your money, health and the people around you. If your relationship is failing, obviously not enough interest is being paid.

"Discipline is the last piece in the Power of Appreciation because if you are smiling while you study then it is easy to focus on what is interesting to you. With all of that then you would not need the discipline to keep going. But sometimes discipline is necessary to get back on track.

"Before I end I want to leave you with this story. When I was young, I would ask my father for many things, as young people do and he would always admonish me for not taking care of or appreciating what I had. And of course, I did not appreciate what he was saying. Later in life before getting my financial soul straight, I was all over the place. Wasting money and time chasing everything and not appreciating what I had.

"When it came time to pull the money together to get married and start a family I was forced to pull together my personal financial statement. Then for the first time in dollars and cents I could see how not appreciating what I had was costing me. More importantly I could see that if I did not develop an attitude of gratitude and get rid of stinking thinking I would be a slave to giving my energy and money to someone else for the rest of my life.

"Many people really like money but do not have the discipline to appreciate it. When they think of it they don't smile, refuse to study, don't stay focused and don't show enough interest. It takes discipline to get the Power of Appreciation going.

"Appreciation is the most powerful builder of wealth in every aspect of your life and you have it in you right now. If you need a reminder, look at babies. You can put a $3000 toy in front of them and they will have just as much fun with the stick they picked up next to it. When you can just appreciate a good time, sometimes money doesn't mean a thing.

"I appreciate you guys coming here today. It is my prayer that you take advantage of the lessons you can learn at the Financial Soul Institute and that you will take the time to appreciate yourselves because you are so worth it. Thank you."

With that Rev. Simmons took a step over to shake Sarah's hand but she opened her arms wide and gave him hug as the sound of applause rose from around the room. Then Doris stood up clapping followed by others until there was a moving standing ovation from the front and into the overflow area.

Rev. Simmons turned to wave and acknowledges the crowd. Even from the screens in the overflow room it was obvious that he was tearing up which lead to an even more raucous standing ovation with shouts of "Alright Rev. Simmons ...Yeah!"

Then Sarah took to the center of the stage, while clapping with the audience. As the applause subsided she said, "I really don't think there is anything else that can be added here today. Thank you for your enlightenment Rev. Simmons. Please remember to continue to look for ways to appreciate your money by studying it.

"Thank you everyone. I hope to see you all again next time."

Chapter 10

Financial Friendships

Back in Mr. Robert's office the mood was festive. Ed, Rev. Simmons, Mr. Roberts, Bobby and his father Ken stood together laughing and poking fun at Mr. Roberts calling him an old retired softy.

Sarah and Sasha stood off to the side chatting. Sasha excitedly asked in a low whisper. "So…are you two guys getting back together?"

"It is one day at a time but after seeing you and Ed it reminded me of where we started", Sarah answered. "How we had dreams of a family. But unlike you guys we did not look for financial help before expanding our little family business. We walked in blind and got blind sided.

"I think we now fully appreciate that most of our problems were about money. Now that I have a handle of my own financial philosophy and he is willing to learn with me, I think we have a chance. But our arguments got really heated so we have some healing to take care of."

Sasha looked over at Ken holding Bobby. Then her eyes drifted over to Ed. "I really don't want to go down that road. Money is a really personal issue. When you are taught all of your life to go out and make money, then it can become a measuring stick of your success. If you are not making it or worse you can not keep it, then you feel like a failure and you really don't want other people to go poking into your failures."

"That is why the Financial Soul Institute teaches people that uneducated debt is not their fault but educated wealth is their destiny", Sarah said as she watched Bobby and Ken play together. "Back in the day there were kings and queens that watched out for the people, during the industrial age the companies took care of the people and now during the information and financial knowledge age people have to take care of themselves.

"The information age has been here for just one generation. The financial knowledge age is just getting started. No one saw it coming. Not the schools or your parents. Everyone just blindly went along thinking everything would be OK...even if you messed up...and this is not the case anymore.

Sarah looked Sasha in the eyes and said, "You guys are doing the right things. You are looking for mentors, attending seminars and actively seeking answers. Some people just bury their heads and dream that someday it will be ok...and sadly it won't."

Rev. Simmons called over to Sasha and Sarah, "Hey ladies. Ed just asked a great question and I want you to hear it. Go ahead Ed, ask that again.

Ed cleared his throat and repeated, "I was asking Mr. Roberts if he lost all of his money tomorrow and he had to start all over what he would do differently?"

"Oh that is an easy one huh Reverend?" said Mr. Roberts. "I would go right into network marketing or as I like to call Financial Friendships".

Sasha looked alarmed. "You would join a pyramid scheme?"

"Oh God...here we go", sighed Mr. Roberts. "Uh...sorry Rev. Actually little lady, since you are a government contractor you are technically in a pyramid scheme".

"What? I don't understand", said Sasha.

Rev. Simmons explained, "Your manager gets paid more than you right? And her manager gets paid more than she does. And that manager gets paid more and it keeps going up until the person at the top gets paid the most. That makes a nice little pyramid...even in the corporate world. Isn't that right John?

"Just call me King Tut little buddy", Mr. Roberts snickered. "Corporations are really pyramid schemes with one person on the top. A true network marketing business is the exact opposite of a traditional business model because it is designed to bring you up to the top, not keep you down at the bottom. It does not succeed unless you bring people to the top."

"Network marketing has gotten a bad rap for a couple of reasons", continued the Reverend. "Most people just don't understand it and others think that you are just selling which they fear."

"But the truth of the matter is that it is one of the best ways for someone with little or no experience to create their own business and make a great deal of money in their spare time. Even Donald Trump endorses it as a great way to gain wealth. There are now even classes in it at the top ranked Ivy League schools."

"As you know, most of our schools are set up to teach you how to get a job so the concept of network marketing is foreign to most people but truthfully it is the best way to sell a product or service because it works by word of mouth". The Reverend turned to Ed and asked, "Now Ed…if you were to launch a new product, what would be your biggest concern?"

Without hesitating Ed replied, "Paying for the marketing. Your cash flow will be non existent if people don't know you have a product for them to buy."

"That's right", exclaimed Mr. Roberts. "So instead of paying thousands for an ad agency to make the ads and then paying even more for every time the ad is run, you let a network of people do the marketing for you. The great thing is you aren't paying the money for marketing up front…only when the product is sold."

Mr. Roberts rubbed his hands together excitedly and said, "In network marketing all of that ad money is given to the people in the network for marketing it. Now here is where the magic comes in. It is called passive income which basically means you get paid for work you did sometime in the past.

"With passive income in network marketing, once you have set up an organization that works with you to increase the number of people who purchase your product or service monthly, you receive income based on the production of the people in your organization."

"The great thing about passive income is that you can get paid whether you are still working or not. Even if you moved to another location your passive income follows you. You can even pass this along to your kids when you die so they can manage your network and keep the passive income rolling along. You can't do that with a job."

"You can also begin to gain the tax advantages of the rich. A person with a part-time business can take more tax deductions than an employee can. For example, you may be able to deduct car expenses, gasoline, some meals and entertainment. You can't do that as an employee."

"It does take time to build your own network but it does not take a lot for you to get in.

You get to work, learn, teach and be around like minded individuals who want you to succeed. The systems are already in place for you and are proven to work which frees you to build your network and not build the accounting, shipping or anything else.

"In other words, all the work of setting up a business is done for you but you get to grow the business on your own terms", the Reverend added.

Ed asked, "What did you mean when you called it financial friendships?"

"What is the one thing that I can guarantee that everyone in this room will do in the next two days? The answer is spending money. Now who is this money going to? Are they friends of yours or are you sending your money to people you don't know and who really don't care about you.

"We are all friends here and we have some spending in common. So why not work within a system that allows us to support each other financially? Your business is now empowering your friends and your community by keeping the money circulating with each other. The more friends you have in your network, the more money for everyone. It is not selling, it simply making friends and supporting each other financially."

"I can testify to that", said Ken. "I was really skeptical about it but Sarah has been building her network of friends and there is no denying the checks that she is making. I just signed up under her and she has been coaching me."

"That's right", said Sarah excitedly. "I went to part time with my job last month and I plan to be retiring from there in three months. At the pace I am on right now, I will have increased my income by 80% in my first year."

At that moment Mr. Roberts looked at his watch, jumped up and ran over to his desk while his voice boomed out over the room, "Ok everybody...gather around. We have a ceremony to get ready for. Time is a tickin'. You two kids get over here."

Rev. Simmons grabbed Ed and Sasha and pulled them in front of Mr. Roberts' desk. Sarah clapped excitedly as she pushed a bewildered Ken over to the side in what was beginning to look like a wedding formation.

Mr. Roberts stood on the side of his desk as Rev. Simmons stood in front of the desk facing Ed and Sasha who just grinned in anticipation. Mr. Roberts picked up a remote control and turned on a CD that played solemn classical music.

Rev. Simmons cleared his throat, gathered himself and spoke loudly as if the room was crowded. "Ladies, gentlemen and little boy geniuses", the Reverend said winking at Bobby who just giggled. "Today we celebrate the successful completion of the…"

"Money boot camp", Mr. Roberts shouted with his feigned southern accent as he saluted while standing at full attention.

Rev. Simmons looked at him, rolled his eyes and continued, "Yes, yes the money boot camp. You came to us seeking your millions but we hope you leave here with something that has more value. The knowledge that you have gained here is not just for you. It is for your children, your families, your communities and to be used for the rest of your lives."

"Wealth is not just about the number of zeros in your bank account. It is not about the number of dead presidents on pieces of paper that you possess. Wealth is about living in appreciation. Living in appreciation of what you have worked for, the people around you and most importantly an appreciation for giving."

"Amen", shouted Mr. Roberts. Sarah raised her hand and shouted, "That's right Reverend…take your time!"

Rev. Simmons continued with his voice rising. "Your financial soul is connected to your mind, body and spirit. If you do not take care of one you will falter with the other. Do not let your lives be consumed by being a consumer. Do not give your time and energy away and not have anything left for your mind, body and spirit.

"The story of Adam and Eve in the garden showed us that it is more important to appreciate what you have than to be so greedy as to go after what has not been promised to you. If you try to have everything then you won't appreciate anything and you will end up with nothing.

"Woo…my, my, my preach Reverend", shouted Ken to the surprise of Mr. Roberts and Sarah.

"You came to us with heavy financial souls. Hopefully we have given you the insight to lift your own spirits. A financial education is the only cure for the financially broken soul. Remember the world owes you nothing…it was here first."

"And now", Rev. Simmons continued, "We need to ask you a few questions to make sure you are ready for the world. And please, any little boy geniuses in the room must hold their answers". Bobby giggled again.

"What is the secret of money?"

"Compound interest", replied Ed.

"Great", Rev. Simmons enthused. "What is the secret of business?"

"Care about people," Sasha answered quickly.

Mr. Roberts asked, "And what is the secret of real estate?"

"Leverage", said Ed.

Rev. Simmons shot back with, "How about the secret to investing?"

"Take the time to develop a long term plan that you can follow", answered Sasha.

"Well done", Rev. Simmons encouraged. "So what is the secret of personal financial success?"

"Reading financial statements", said Ed and Sasha together.

Mr. Roberts asked, "Do you know who gets a constantly updated financial statement on you that are read by professionals?"

Ed turned, winked at Bobby and said, "The credit bureau".

"Excellent", said Mr. Roberts. "What is the secret of great wealth?"

Ed and Sasha looked at each other and said, "Appreciation."

"And the secret to appreciation is smiling", offered Sasha.

Rev. Simmons looked at Mr. Roberts and said, "I think our students are ready for graduation."

Mr. Roberts picked up two nicely bowed rolled up sheets of parchment paper and handed them to Ed and Sasha while shaking their hands. Rev. Simmons said congratulation and instructed them to take the bows off the papers and read them.

Ed and Sasha slipped the bows off and unfurled the paper. With a surprised look on their faces they looked each others sheets.

"There has been a mistake", said Ed, "These sheets are blank."

Rev. Simmons, Mr. Roberts and Sarah all started laughing. Mr. Roberts was doubled over in laughter and managed, "We got them again. Ooooh. Did you see the looks on their faces? That was too easy."

Sasha looked at Sarah who had her hand over her mouth as she tried to hold in her laughter. "You were in on this too? Why didn't you warn me?"

"I'm sorry. They did it to me too. But you guys did fall for it hard", she said leaning on Ken for support.

"Sorry kids", said the Reverend while trying to compose himself. "This isn't some fancy school where you graduate for just learning."

"Yeah, welcome to the real world baby. You have to do something and get positive results to win out here", Mr. Roberts chimed in. "When you can create your own personal financial statement and you can read it…then and only then will you graduate."

Rev. Simmons looked at his watch and said, "Uh-oh, I am going to be late." Then he took off out of the room leaving Ed and Sasha stunned and dazed.

Sasha stumbled over to the couch and plopped down. "I'm going to miss you guys. It may not be today but at some point…"

Sarah smiled, sat down next to her and took her hand. "Hey you have to pay a price for everything. At least with these guys your price is everybody around you is always laughing."

"You know what you are right", Sasha said perking up. Then she popped up out of the seat and ran over to Mr. Roberts and gave him a hug. "We really appreciate you guys taking the time to teach us."

"Yeah. This has definitely been a learning experience", said Ed as he stared at the blank sheets of paper.

"It was our pleasure", said Mr. Roberts who looked like he was about to blush. Suddenly he looked at his watch. "Uh-oh gotta go", he whispered. His huge frame tip-toeing quickly toward the door looked near cartoonish.

Everyone left in the room just looked at each other in silence. Then in the front janitor room they heard voices then a yell followed by shouting and more laughter. The door sprang open with Rev. Simmons and Mr. Roberts spilling into the room laughing like third grade boys followed by Doris, Michelle and Cathy who all looked red faced.

Sarah walked over to them, smiled and said, "Welcome to the money boot camp ladies. Don't worry the jokes do get worse from here. But it is a financial soul saving experience you can appreciate."

Made in the USA